BETTER THAN THEM

LIFT. LOVE. LEAD. LET GO OF JUDGMENT

BY

SYAVIHA MULENGYA

This book is a gift

From:_____

To:_____

On:_____

Personal Comments

_____

_____

_____

_____

_____

Thank you God for your goodness, grace and the gift you have bestowed upon me

DEDICATION

- To my late parents, Samuel Mahamba and Elizabeth Vahingania, thank you for loving, listening and leading me in the ways of God.

- My brothers and sisters, Moise, Samson, Schandrack, Semu, Seriba, Yerusi, Desize, Kahambu and Katungu Mulengya, thank you for teaching me the values of hope, humility and hard work.

- To my mentors, Janine and Sid Phillips, thank you for your inspiration, instruction and information. You always encourage and believe in my vision.

- To Devin and Christine Walker, you have motivated me to serve, seek and stay close to God. Thank you for your wisdom and the great work you are doing.

- To my queen Rafiki Kavuya Syaviha, thank you for standing, supporting and serving with me in hard and good times. You are my miracle.

- To my lovely daughters, Blessed and Best and Brilliance, you always encourage, excite and enjoy my work. You are my greatest inspiration.

- To my friends and fans, you always advise, appreciate and assist me in this noble work. Thank you for the financial support.

Table of Content

INTRODUCTION

Stop Judging, Start Loving

Life is a journey, and none of us walks it perfectly. Each of us carries a unique blend of strengths and weaknesses, victories and failures, wisdom and mistakes. Yet, despite this shared human experience, society often teaches us to judge—to measure others against unrealistic standards, to compare, and to elevate some while diminishing others. But imagine a world where we choose a different path. Imagine a life where judgment is replaced by kindness, where people lift each other up rather than tear each other down. The truth is simple: No one is superior, and no one is beneath anyone else. We are all human and worthy of love and respect.

Too often, people feel the need to boast about their successes or to criticize others' shortcomings. They believe their value is tied to their accomplishments, possessions, or status. But true greatness is not found in bragging or judgment—it is found in humility. The strongest people are not those who stand on pedestals but those who extend their hands to help others rise. When we recognize that every person has value, regardless of their struggles or strengths, we begin to see the world through a lens of compassion rather than competition.

SYAVIHA MULENGYA

Love has the power to heal, to transform, to inspire. It teaches us to lead with understanding rather than assumption, to embrace differences rather than fear them. When we love, we stop seeing flaws as reasons to reject people and start recognizing them as reminders that we are all human. Instead of using weaknesses as excuses to judge, we can use them as opportunities to connect—to build bridges where there were once barriers, to offer encouragement instead of condemnation. The most meaningful relationships are built not on perfection but on acceptance, patience, and care.

This book is an invitation to shift your mindset and open your heart. It is a reminder that we are all imperfect, yet we are all deeply deserving of kindness. It challenges us to stop judging and start loving, to lift, to lead, to look after one another. The world is already filled with criticism and division, but we have the power to create a new way of living—one built on encouragement, understanding, and true connection. We don't need to prove our worth through arrogance or judgment; we simply need to show up for one another with open hearts and open minds.

So let's choose love over judgment. Let's decide to see the beauty in others rather than their flaws. Let's create a world where compassion is stronger than comparison, where support replaces criticism, and where every person feels seen, valued, and uplifted. A better world isn't built by tearing others down—it is built by lifting each other up. The journey begins now.

SYAVIHA MULENGYA

1

****

NO ONE IS PERFECT

L ife is full of challenges, and **no one** walks this journey without facing struggles. We all have imperfections—things we wish we could change, moments we regret, weaknesses we try to hide. But the truth is, God never asked us to be perfect—He asks us to trust Him, to love Him, and to grow in faith. The Bible reminds us in **Romans 3:23**, *"For all have sinned and fall short of the glory of God."* This is not a verse of condemnation, but of truth and freedom. It reminds us that no one is flawless, but in Christ, we are forgiven and loved beyond measure.

No One Has It All Together

1. Shortcomings: Everyone Has Weaknesses

No one is perfect. Every person has areas where they struggle, habits they wish to change, and qualities they need to improve. Some people battle with impatience, others struggle with fear, and many feel insecure about their abilities. But weakness does not make us unworthy; it makes us human. God does No one is perfect—we all have weaknesses, failures, and shortcomings. It is easy to compare ourselves with others, thinking they are better or stronger. But everyone has struggles, even if we do not see them.

Instead of letting pride control us, we should accept our imperfections and show love to others. When we stop comparing and start appreciating ourselves and others, we find true strength in kindness and humility. As **Romans 12:3** reminds us, *"Do not think of yourself more highly than you ought, but rather think of yourself with sober judgment."*

Many people try to hide their flaws because they fear rejection or judgment. They pretend to be strong when they feel weak or act confident when they feel unsure. But hiding our struggles does not make them go away—it only adds more pressure. God does not expect us to be perfect; He simply wants us to come to Him with an open heart. In **2 Corinthians 12:9**, He says, *"My grace is sufficient for you, for My power is made perfect in weakness."* Instead of running from our shortcomings, we can trust that His grace will lift us up.

Recognizing our weaknesses should not make us feel defeated. Instead, it should remind us to be humble and compassionate toward others. We all struggle in different ways, and that is why we need each other. When we stop trying to be superior and instead focus on love and acceptance, we can build stronger relationships and live in peace. **Philippians 2:3** tells us, *"Do nothing out of selfish ambition or vain conceit. Rather, in humility value others above yourselves."*

Letting go of pride and embracing both our strengths and weaknesses allows us to grow. We do not need to prove ourselves to anyone or compete to be the best. When we stop comparing and start loving, we create space for joy, peace, and deeper faith. God does not ask for perfection—He asks for a willing heart. When we surrender to Him, He works through us, turning our struggles into strengths. **James 4:10** beautifully expresses this truth: *"Humble yourselves before the Lord, and He will lift you up."*

2. Struggles

Struggles are a part of life, and no one is exempt from them. Everyone, regardless of background, status, or success, faces battles—some are visible, while others are hidden deep in the heart. These difficulties remind us that we are human and that we need each other. Life is not meant to be lived alone, and struggles teach us that community and support are essential.

When we go through hardships, we should never feel ashamed. Struggles do not mean we are weak—they show that we are growing, learning, and becoming stronger. **Galatians 6:2** says, *"Carry each other's burdens, and in this way, you will fulfill the law of Christ."* This verse encourages us to stand with others in their pain and to support them rather than judge them. We are called to help one another, lift each other up, and extend love and grace.

Rather than looking down on those who struggle, we should remind them that they are not alone. No one's hardships define them, and everyone deserves kindness. True strength lies in unity, in choosing compassion over judgment, and in being a source of encouragement to those in need.

3. Setbacks

Life is full of setbacks. Dreams are delayed, mistakes happen, and plans fall apart. These disappointments can sometimes make us feel like failures, but setbacks are not the end—they are opportunities to grow, learn, and trust in God's plan. Instead of feeling discouraged, we should see setbacks as stepping stones toward greater wisdom and maturity.

When we experience obstacles, we should not lose hope. **Philippians 4:13** reminds us, *"I can do all things through Him who gives me strength."* This verse teaches us that even when life does not go as planned, we can find strength in God. He is always there to guide us through difficult moments and to turn challenges into growth. Instead of letting failure define us, we should trust that God is using setbacks for a greater purpose.

Rather than judging others for their struggles, we should encourage them to keep going. We should remind them that setbacks do not mean they are unworthy or incapable—they are simply part of life's journey. Strength is not measured by avoiding failure but by the ability to rise again, learn, and keep moving forward.

4. Stress

Stress is something everyone faces. Whether from responsibilities, pressure, or expectations, it can be overwhelming. But stress should never control us—it should remind us to lean on God and support one another. Instead of allowing stress to pull us away from people, we should use it as an opportunity to build deeper connections and find peace through support.

The Bible encourages rest and trust in God. **Matthew 11:28** says, *"Come to me, all you who are weary and burdened, and I will give you rest."* This verse reminds us that God offers peace in times of chaos. Instead of letting stress consume us, we should seek His guidance and trust that He will provide comfort. Stress does not mean failure—it is simply a reminder that we need to rely on God and those who care about us.

We should also be mindful of others' stress. When we see people struggling, we should reach out in kindness. Stress is lighter when shared, and life is easier when we walk together. Instead of competing to be the strongest, we should work together to create a culture of patience, encouragement, and peace.

5. Sin

Sin is a part of human nature. No one is free from making mistakes, failing in their actions, or choosing the wrong path. Understanding this truth should humble us. It should remind us that no one is above anyone else and that we all need grace, forgiveness, and patience. Instead of thinking we are superior or better than others, we should recognize that we all struggle with sin in different ways. Some sins are visible, while others are hidden in the heart. But regardless of how they appear, sin is something we all face.

When we acknowledge our own weaknesses, we learn to extend mercy to others. **Romans 3:23** says, *"For all have sinned and fall short of the glory of God."* This verse makes it clear that none of us is perfect. No one has the right to judge others, because everyone has fallen short in some way. When we understand this, we stop looking down on people for their failures. Instead, we help them rise. We offer encouragement, wisdom, and kindness. We remind them that mistakes do not define them but rather provide opportunities to grow, seek forgiveness, and become better.

True humility comes from knowing that we are all flawed. This realization should not make us feel ashamed but should help us develop compassion. Rather than using our mistakes to condemn ourselves or others, we should allow them to teach us understanding. We should use them to strengthen relationships, to listen without judgment, and to love without conditions. Instead of hiding our faults, we should use them to create deeper connections, reminding each other that we are all on a journey of learning, healing, and growth.

6. Scars

Everyone carries scars. Some are physical, marking moments of pain and injury. Others are emotional, left behind by difficult experiences, heartbreaks, and losses. But scars do not mean we are weak—they are proof that we have survived hardships. They remind us that despite the pain we have endured, we are still standing, still moving forward, and still able to heal.

Instead of hiding our scars, we should embrace them. **Psalm 147:3** says, *"He heals the brokenhearted and binds up their wounds."* This verse reassures us that God does not ignore our pain—He restores and strengthens us. The wounds we once thought would never heal become testimonies of resilience. Scars show that we have overcome obstacles, made it through dark moments, and found the courage to keep going. They are reminders that healing is possible and that we are stronger than our struggles.

We should never judge others for the scars they carry. Instead, we should extend love, understanding, and encouragement. Many people suffer silently, afraid to share their pasts because of judgment. But when we treat them with kindness rather than criticism, we help them find healing. Instead of looking at scars with shame, we should see them as symbols of perseverance. True strength is found in love, in supporting one another, and in reminding each other that we are not alone in our pain.

7. Secrets

Everyone has secrets. Some are personal regrets, while others are painful memories they wish they could forget. Some secrets are carried out of fear—fear of rejection, fear of judgment, or fear that if people knew the truth, they would turn away. But secrets can be heavy burdens. They can create isolation, making people feel disconnected from those around them.

Instead of hiding in shame, we should seek honesty and healing. **James 5:16** says, *"Confess your sins to each other and pray for each other so that you may be healed."* This verse teaches us that there is power in sharing and seeking support. When we open up, we break the chains of fear. We allow healing to begin, and we discover that we are not alone in our struggles. Often, the things we hide are the same things others have faced. And when we choose to be honest, we create space for trust, understanding, and deeper connections.

Being vulnerable takes courage, but it leads to freedom. Instead of letting secrets trap us, we should let honesty bring us peace. We should create an environment where people feel safe to share, knowing they will not be judged but supported. No one should feel alone in their burdens. True healing happens when we replace fear with faith, isolation with love, and secrecy with openness.

8. Self-Doubt

Self-doubt happens to everyone. Sometimes, we feel unsure about ourselves. We wonder whether we are good enough, whether we can succeed, or whether we are important. We look at others and think they are stronger or smarter. But the truth is, even they have moments of doubt. No one is completely confident all the time.

Instead of letting doubt control us, we should remind ourselves that we do not have to be perfect. **Isaiah 41:10** says, *"Do not fear,* *for I am with you; do not be dismayed, for I am your God. I will strengthen you and help you; I will uphold you with my righteous right hand."* This verse teaches us that even in moments of uncertainty, we are not alone. God is with us, and He gives us the strength we need.

Self-doubt does not define us. It is just a feeling, and feelings can change. We should be kind to ourselves and remember that mistakes and failures do not mean we are worthless. Instead of comparing ourselves to others, we should focus on learning, growing, and helping. When we encourage others, we also build our own confidence. True strength comes from trusting God and believing that we are valuable, no matter our weaknesses.

SYAVIHA MULENGYA

2

****

JUDGE LESS, LOVE MORE

Before You Judge, Choose Love

Before judging others, we must stop and reflect. No one is perfect, and we all have struggles. Instead of looking down on others, we should choose to love, lift, and care. **Matthew 7:1-2** says, *"Do not judge, or you too will be judged. For in the same way you judge others, you will be judged."* This verse reminds us that judging others does not make us better—it only separates us from kindness.

Pride often leads to judgment. When we feel superior, we begin to criticize others instead of helping them grow. But true wisdom comes from humility. **Proverbs 16:18** warns, *"Pride goes before destruction, a haughty spirit before a fall."* If we want to make a difference, we must replace judgment with love, patience, and understanding.

Choosing to love instead of judging creates a better world. Imagine if we all encouraged each other instead of pointing out flaws. **Romans 15:7** says, *"Accept one another, then, just as Christ accepted you."* Love is stronger than judgment, and when we lift others, we also lift ourselves.

SYAVIHA MULENGYA

Lift Up, Don't Tear Down

1. Check Yourself

Before judging someone else, we should take a moment to check ourselves. Have we ever made mistakes? Have we struggled in life? The answer is always yes. **Luke 6:41-42** asks, *"Why do you look at the speck of sawdust in your brother's eye and pay no attention to the plank in your own eye?"* This verse teaches us to reflect before criticizing others.

Judgment often comes from pride or insecurity. Sometimes, we judge people because we want to feel better about ourselves. But true strength comes from kindness, not comparison. **James 4:10** reminds us, *"Humble yourselves before the Lord, and He will lift you up."*

Instead of focusing on the flaws of others, we should work on improving ourselves. **Philippians 2:3** says, *"Do nothing out of selfish ambition or vain conceit. Rather, in humility value others above yourselves."* Checking ourselves first helps us grow and makes us more understanding toward others.

2. Correct Your Mistakes

It is easy to judge others, but hard to admit our own mistakes. Many times, people criticize others while ignoring their own flaws. **Romans 3:23** tells us, *"For all have sinned and fall short of the glory of God."* None of us is perfect, so instead of judging, we should focus on correcting our own mistakes.

Mistakes are a part of life, but ignoring them leads to pride. When we admit our faults and seek growth, we become wiser and more compassionate. **Proverbs 28:13** says, *"Whoever conceals their sins does not prosper, but the one who confesses and* *renounces them finds mercy."* Instead of judging others, we should work on becoming better ourselves.

True wisdom comes from learning. If we take time to understand our mistakes, we will be slower to criticize others for theirs. **Matthew 5:7** reminds us, *"Blessed are the merciful, for they will be shown mercy."* Choosing mercy instead of judgment makes life more peaceful and meaningful.

3. Consider

Before forming an opinion about someone, we should take time to consider their situation. Everyone has struggles, and we do not always know what someone is going through. **Ephesians 4:2** says, *"Be completely humble and gentle; be patient, bearing with one another in love."* When we think about a person's journey, we grow in kindness.

Sometimes, people act in ways we do not understand. But instead of judging, we should try to see things from their perspective. **Colossians 3:12** reminds us, *"Clothe yourselves with compassion, kindness, humility, gentleness, and patience."* When we consider others with an open heart, we become more loving.

Taking time to understand people's experiences prevents unfair judgment. **Proverbs 18:13** warns, *"To answer before listening—that is folly and shame."* Listening and considering help us respond with love rather than criticism.

4. Connect

Connection is the key to building relationships and understanding others. Before judging, we should take time to connect with people and learn about their experiences. **Hebrews 10:24-25** says, *"Let us consider how we may spur one another on* *toward love and good deeds, not giving up meeting together, but encouraging one another."* This verse reminds us that true connections come from love, encouragement, and togetherness.

Many times, people judge without truly knowing someone's story. They assume things based on appearance, status, or past mistakes. But when we take time to listen, we gain insight into their struggles, victories, and dreams. **Proverbs 18:13** warns, *"To answer before listening—that is folly and shame."* Connecting with people means understanding them, and understanding leads to kindness.

Strong connections build trust. When we engage with others, we create a space where people feel valued. Instead of pushing people away, we should welcome them in. **Romans 15:7** tells us, *"Accept one another, then, just as Christ accepted you."* Connection is about seeing the worth in everyone, regardless of their background.

Building relationships also strengthens our own hearts. When we choose to understand rather than judge, we open ourselves up to love and wisdom. **Colossians 3:14** says, *"And over all these virtues put on love, which binds them all together in perfect unity."* Connection creates unity, bringing people closer instead of dividing them.

True connection transforms lives. It teaches us patience, kindness, and empathy. Instead of judging people, we should look at them with understanding. **Galatians 6:2** reminds us, *"Carry each other's burdens, and in this way, you will fulfill the law of Christ."* By connecting, we create a world filled with love and acceptance.

5. Clarify

Judgment often comes from misunderstanding. Before forming an opinion about someone, we should take time to clarify the situation. **Proverbs 2:6** says, *"For the Lord gives wisdom; from His mouth come knowledge and understanding."* Seeking clarity helps us respond with wisdom instead of assumptions.

Many people are quick to judge before knowing the full story. They jump to conclusions based on limited information, causing unnecessary hurt and division. But clarity allows us to see things as they truly are. **James 1:19** teaches, *"Everyone should be quick to listen, slow to speak, and slow to become angry."* Taking time to understand first leads to more loving relationships.

Clarifying also prevents conflict. When we ask questions instead of assuming, we build trust and create meaningful connections. **Proverbs 15:1** tells us, "A gentle answer turns away wrath, but a harsh word stirs up anger." When we take time to understand, we approach situations with grace rather than harshness.

Seeking clarity strengthens wisdom. Instead of letting emotions guide our opinions, we should focus on truth and understanding. **Ecclesiastes 7:9** warns, *"Do not be quickly provoked in your spirit, for anger resides in the lap of fools."* A patient and thoughtful heart creates peace instead of division. Clarification leads to love. When we stop judging and start listening, we build bridges instead of walls. **Ephesians 4:2** reminds us, *"Be completely humble; be patient, bearing with one another in love."* True relationships thrive when we replace assumptions with understanding.

6. Celebrate

Celebration is about recognizing the good in life, appreciating people, and expressing joy for achievements—big or small. We should celebrate not only ourselves but also others. **Psalm 118:24** says, "*This is the day that the Lord has made; let us rejoice and be glad in it.*" Each day is a blessing, and taking time to celebrate makes life more meaningful.

Many times, people focus on problems instead of victories. They complain about what they lack rather than appreciating what they have. But celebration teaches gratitude. **1 Thessalonians 5:16-18** says, "*Rejoice always, pray continually, give thanks in all circumstances.*" When we choose joy, we create a positive and uplifting environment.

Celebrating others is just as important as celebrating ourselves. Instead of competing, we should encourage people when they succeed. A world where people cheer each other on is a world of love, not jealousy. **Romans 12:10** reminds us, "*Be devoted to one another in love. Honor one another above yourselves.*" True celebration happens when we lift others up.

Celebration strengthens relationships. When we appreciate people's efforts, they feel valued and respected. **Hebrews 10:24-25** says, "*Let us consider how we may spur one another on toward love and good deeds.*" A simple word of encouragement can bring hope and inspire confidence.

Life is full of reasons to celebrate. It could be a new opportunity, a small achievement, or simply the gift of a new day. Choosing to celebrate creates joy, strengthens communities, and reminds people that they matter. **Ecclesiastes 3:12** says, "*I know that there is nothing better for people than to be happy and to do good while they live.*" Celebration is a way of spreading love and making life brighter.

SYAVIHA MULENGYA

7. Cherish

Cherishing means valuing people, moments, and relationships. It is about recognizing the importance of those around us and treating them with kindness. **Proverbs 17:17** says, *"A friend loves at all times, and a brother is born for a time of adversity."* Cherishing people strengthens our connections and helps us create lasting bonds.

Many people take relationships for granted. They assume that friends, family, and loved ones will always be there. But life changes quickly, and time is precious. **Ephesians 4:2** reminds us, *"Be completely humble and gentle; be patient, bearing with one another in love."* When we cherish people, we appreciate their presence, respect their feelings, and value their role in our lives.

Cherishing does not just mean saying "I care"—it means showing it through actions. A small gesture, a kind word, or a moment of listening can make a difference. **Colossians 3:14** says, *"Over all these virtues put on love, which binds them all together in perfect unity."* Choosing to cherish people builds trust, deepens relationships, and spreads love.

When we cherish the moments we share, we create memories that last forever. Instead of focusing on stress, we should enjoy the little things—laughter, friendship, and love. **James 1:17** reminds us, *"Every good and perfect gift is from above."* Life is a gift, and cherishing it makes every moment worthwhile.

True happiness comes from valuing others and treating them with care. When we cherish people, we create a world where love is stronger than judgment. **John 13:34** says, *"Love one another. As I have loved you, so you must love one another."* Cherishing means choosing kindness, embracing gratitude, and making every relationship meaningful.

3

******

SOW WHAT
YOU WANT TO REAP

Do to Others What You Expect Them to Do for You

Life is like a mirror—it reflects back what we give to others. If we want to be loved, we must first show love. If we desire kindness, we must first be kind. If we hope for respect, we must respect others. Many times, people wish to be treated with dignity, yet they fail to treat others the same way. This is why we must remember the golden rule: **Luke 6:31** says, *"Do to others as you would have them do to you."* This means we must treat people the way we would like to be treated. Instead of waiting for people to be good to us, we must take the first step and be good to them.

It is easy to demand fairness, yet hard to give it. Many people want others to be honest, patient, and understanding with them, but they fail to extend these qualities in return. If we want a world filled with love and peace, we must create it through our own actions. People learn by example. If we want to receive kindness, we must practice kindness. If we expect generosity, we should give freely. **Galatians 6:7** reminds us, *"A man reaps what he sows."* This means that whatever we plant in the lives of others—love, encouragement, or peace—will eventually grow and return to us.

Life needs good people—people willing to lead by example. If we believe in kindness, we must practice kindness. If we value respect, we must show respect to others first. **Romans 12:21** teaches us, "*Do not be overcome by evil, but overcome evil with good.*" This reminds us that the best way to fight negativity is by spreading goodness. Instead of judging people for their mistakes, we should lift them up and encourage them. The way we treat others speaks louder than words. Our actions should match what we believe, and through love and compassion, we can inspire others to do the same.

How to Set a Good Example: Treat Others the Way You Want to Be Treated

The way we treat others reflects who we are. If we want kindness, respect, and love, we must first show these qualities ourselves. **Luke 6:31** says, "*Do to others as you would have them do to you.*" This means that before expecting good treatment from others, we must be willing to give it. Setting a good example is not just about words—it is about actions. People learn from what they see, and when we treat others well, we inspire them to do the same.

Many times, people demand respect but fail to give it. They want others to listen, care, and be patient, yet they do not practice these things themselves. If we want a world filled with kindness, we must create it through our own behavior. **Galatians 6:7** reminds us, "*A man reaps what he sows.*" This means that whatever we give— whether love, patience, or understanding—will come back to us. If we want peace, we must spread peace. If we want love, we must show love.

SYAVIHA MULENGYA

Life needs good people—people who lead by example. **Romans 12:21** teaches us, *"Do not be overcome by evil, but overcome evil with good."* Instead of complaining about the wrongs in the world, we must strive to bring goodness wherever we go. The best way to teach others how to treat us is to treat them with dignity and love. When our words match our actions, we become true examples of wisdom and grace.

1. Treat Them Well

Treating others well is the foundation of good relationships. If we want kindness, we must first be kind. If we want respect, we must first show respect. **Matthew 7:12** says, *"So in everything, do to others what you would have them do to you."* This verse reminds us that how we treat others shapes how they treat us.

Many times, people expect fairness but fail to give it. They want others to be patient, understanding, and generous, yet they do not practice these qualities themselves. If we want a world filled with love and peace, we must create it through our own actions. **Proverbs 11:17** says, *"Those who are kind benefit themselves, but the cruel bring ruin on themselves."* This means that kindness not only helps others but also brings blessings to our own lives.

Life is about relationships, and relationships grow stronger when we treat people with care. Instead of judging others for their mistakes, we should lift them up and encourage them. The way we treat others speaks louder than words. Our actions should match what we believe, and through love and compassion, we can inspire others to do the same.

2. Think Right

Our thoughts shape our actions. If we think negatively about others, we will treat them poorly. If we think with love and understanding, we will act with kindness. **Philippians 4:8** says, *"Whatever is true, whatever is noble, whatever is right, whatever is pure, whatever is lovely, whatever is admirable—think about such things."* This verse teaches us to focus on good thoughts because good thoughts lead to good actions.

Many times, people assume the worst about others. They judge quickly, criticize harshly, and fail to see the good in people. But if we want to be treated kindly, we must first think kindly of others. **Proverbs 23:7** says, *"As a man thinks in his heart, so is he."* This means that our thoughts shape who we are. If we fill our minds with love, patience, and understanding, we will naturally treat others with respect.

Thinking right also means giving people the benefit of the doubt. Instead of assuming the worst, we should choose to believe in their goodness. When we think positively, we create a world where kindness and love grow. Our thoughts influence our words and actions, and when we think with wisdom, we set a good example for others.

3. Talk Nicely

Words have power. They can build people up or tear them down. **Proverbs 18:21** says, *"The tongue has the power of life and death."* This means that the way we speak can bring life, encouragement, and healing, or it can bring pain and destruction. If we want others to speak kindly to us, we must first speak kindly to them.

SYAVIHA MULENGYA

Many times, people demand respect but use harsh words. They want others to listen, but they speak without care. If we want to be treated with kindness, we must first practice kindness in our speech. **Ephesians 4:29** says, *"Do not let any unwholesome talk come out of your mouths, but only what is helpful for building others up."* This verse reminds us that our words should encourage, not harm.

Talking nicely means choosing words that bring peace. Instead of arguing, we should seek understanding. Instead of criticizing, we should offer encouragement. When we speak with love, we create an atmosphere of respect and kindness. Our words should reflect the goodness in our hearts, and when we speak wisely, we inspire others to do the same.

4. Trust

Trust is the foundation of strong relationships. It allows people to feel safe, valued, and respected. If we want others to trust us, we must first show that we are trustworthy. **Proverbs 3:5** says, *"Trust in the Lord with all your heart and lean not on your own understanding."* This verse reminds us that trust is built on faith, honesty, and reliability. When we treat others with sincerity, they will feel comfortable trusting us in return.

Many times, people expect trust but fail to give it. They want others to believe in them, yet they do not show honesty or dependability. Trust is not something that happens instantly—it grows over time through actions. **Luke 16:10** says, *"Whoever can be trusted with very little can also be trusted with much."* This means that even small acts of honesty and reliability matter. If we want people to trust us, we must be consistent in our words and actions.

Trust also means believing in others. Instead of doubting or assuming the worst, we should give people the benefit of the doubt. **1 Corinthians 13:7** says, *"Love always protects, always trusts, always hopes, always perseveres."* When we trust others, we show them that we value their character. Trust strengthens relationships, builds unity, and creates a world where people feel safe and respected.

5. Touch

A simple touch can bring comfort, healing, and reassurance. Whether it is a handshake, a hug, or a gentle pat on the back, touch has the power to connect people. **Mark 10:16** says, *"And he took the children in his arms, placed his hands on them and blessed them."* Jesus used touch to show love and care, reminding us that physical connection can bring peace and encouragement.

Many times, people feel alone and disconnected. A kind touch can remind them that they are not alone. **Matthew 8:3** says, *"Jesus reached out his hand and touched the man. 'I am willing,' he said. 'Be clean!'"* This verse shows that touch can bring healing and hope. When we reach out to others with kindness, we help them feel valued and supported.

Touch also expresses love and friendship. A warm embrace can comfort someone in pain, and a reassuring hand can give strength to those who feel weak. **Ecclesiastes 4:9-10** says, *"Two are better than one... If either of them falls down, one can help the other up."* This reminds us that human connection is important. When we use touch to show care, we bring warmth and love into others' lives.

6. Take Care

Taking care of others is a sign of love and responsibility. If we want others to care for us, we must first show care for them.

SYAVIHA MULENGYA

Philippians 2:4 says, *"Let each of you look not only to his own interests, but also to the interests of others."* This verse teaches us that life is not just about ourselves—it is about helping and supporting those around us.

Many times, people expect kindness but fail to give it. They want others to be there for them, yet they do not offer the same in return. **Galatians 6:2** says, *"Carry each other's burdens, and in this way, you will fulfill the law of Christ."* This means that we should help others in their struggles, just as we hope they will help us in ours. Taking care of others is not a duty—it is an act of love.

Caring for others also means being present. Sometimes, people do not need advice or solutions—they just need someone to listen and stand by them. **Romans 12:10** says, *"Be devoted to one another in love. Honor one another above yourselves."* When we take care of others, we create a world where love and kindness grow.

7. Treasure

Treasure is not just about material things—it is about valuing people, relationships, and moments. If we want others to treasure us, we must first treasure them. **Matthew 6:21** says, *"For where your treasure is, there your heart will be also."* This verse reminds us that what we value shapes our lives. When we treasure people, we show them that they are important and loved.

Many times, people take relationships for granted. They expect love and loyalty but fail to appreciate those who give it. **Proverbs 17:17** says, *"A friend loves at all times, and a brother is born for a time of adversity."* This means that true relationships are built on love and commitment. If we want lasting friendships, we must cherish and nurture them.

Treasure also means gratitude. Instead of focusing on what we lack, we should appreciate what we have. **1 Thessalonians 5:18** says, *"Give thanks in all circumstances; for this is God's will for you in Christ Jesus."* When we treasure the people in our lives, we create a world filled with love, appreciation, and joy.

SYAVIHA MULENGYA

4

****

WE ARE ONE

We Complete Each Other

No one is meant to walk through life alone. We need each other to grow, to learn, and to overcome challenges. Every person has strengths and weaknesses, and together we balance each other out. Instead of judging or looking down on others, we should recognize that we are all connected. **Romans 12:4-5** says, *"For just as each of us has one body with many members, and these members do not all have the same function, so in Christ, we, though many, form one body, and each member belongs to all the others."* This verse reminds us that we are all part of something greater, and we complete each other.

When we understand that we are one, we stop competing and start collaborating. We stop comparing and start appreciating. Life is not about proving who is better—it is about lifting each other up. No one is perfect, and no one has all the answers. That is why we need unity, kindness, and support. Instead of tearing people down, we should build them up. Instead of ignoring those in need, we should reach out and help.

We complete each other by sharing love, wisdom, and encouragement. When one person is weak, another can be strong. **When one person is struggling, another can offer guidance**. **Ecclesiastes 4:9-10** says, "*Two are better than one... If either of them falls down, one can help the other up.*" This is why we must stand together, support one another, and create a world where love is stronger than judgment.

1. Collaboration

Collaboration is one of the strongest forces that brings people together. It is about sharing ideas, working toward common goals, and helping each other succeed. No one can accomplish everything alone, and life is richer when we support one another. **1 Corinthians 12:12** tells us, "*For just as the body is one and has many members, and all the members of the body, though many, are one body, so it is with Christ.*" This means that every person plays a role in the bigger picture—we are meant to unite, not divide. Each of us has strengths and weaknesses, but when we collaborate, we build something stronger than what we could ever achieve alone.

Many people believe they have to do everything by themselves. They think asking for help makes them weak, or they feel they cannot depend on others. But true strength comes from unity. When we work together, we learn from each other, we grow, and we become better. **Proverbs 27:17** says, "*As iron sharpens iron, so one person sharpens another.*" This reminds us that through collaboration, we refine our skills, strengthen our knowledge, and improve as individuals. Working together does not mean losing independence—it means using our unique abilities to create something meaningful.

Instead of competing, we should cooperate. Many times, people focus on proving they are better than others. They compare

SYAVIHA MULENGYA

their achievements, skills, or status, forgetting that true success comes from lifting others up. No one is meant to stand alone—we are meant to stand together. **Ecclesiastes 4:9** says, "*Two are better than one because they have a good return for their labor.*" Collaboration increases our potential, allows us to achieve more, and creates opportunities for growth that would not exist if we worked alone.

Collaboration is more than teamwork—it is about creating a supportive environment where everyone feels valued. When we share knowledge, offer encouragement, and work toward common goals, we build communities that thrive. Instead of tearing others down, we should lift them up. **Galatians 6:2** reminds us, "*Carry each other's burdens, and in this way, you will fulfill the law of Christ.*" Helping others does not weaken us—it strengthens the bond we share and allows us all to succeed.

A world built on collaboration is a world of progress. When people come together in unity, they create change, inspire greatness, and transform lives. It is not about proving superiority, but about learning, growing, and helping others rise. **Romans 15:5-6** says, "*May the God who gives endurance and encouragement give you the same attitude of mind toward each other that Christ Jesus had, so that with one mind and one voice you may glorify the God and Father of our Lord Jesus Christ.*" This verse teaches that unity is a reflection of love, and when we choose to work together, we strengthen our relationships and build a better future

2. Compassion

Compassion is the ability to see someone's pain and respond with kindness. It is about understanding that everyone struggles and choosing to help instead of judge. **Colossians 3:12** says,

"Therefore, as God's chosen people, holy and dearly loved, clothe yourselves with compassion, kindness, humility, gentleness, and patience." This verse teaches us that compassion is a choice, and we must practice it daily.

Many times, people are quick to criticize but slow to show mercy. They see someone struggling and assume the worst, rather than offering help. But true compassion means looking beyond mistakes and seeing a person's heart. **Luke 6:36** says, *"Be merciful, just as your Father is merciful."* This reminds us that just as God shows us mercy, we should show mercy to others.

Compassion creates a world where people feel safe, valued, and loved. ***When we choose kindness over judgment, we bring healing instead of harm.*** Instead of ignoring those in need, we should reach out and offer support. True strength is found in love, and when we practice compassion, we make the world a better place.

3. Community

Community is about belonging. It is about knowing that we are not alone, that we are part of something bigger than ourselves. Life is not meant to be lived in isolation—we need each other. **Hebrews 10:24-25** says, *"And let us consider how we may spur one another on toward love and good deeds, not giving up meeting together, but encouraging one another."* This reminds us that relationships and connections give life meaning. When we surround ourselves with people who support, love, and encourage us, we build a world where everyone feels valued.

Many people struggle in silence, feeling that they must face life's difficulties alone. Some fear asking for help, thinking it makes them weak. But the truth is, we are stronger together. **Acts 2:44-45**

SYAVIHA MULENGYA

tells us, *"All the believers were together and had everything in common. They sold property and possessions to give to anyone who had need."* This verse teaches us that true community is about sharing, giving, and lifting each other up. Instead of competing, we should collaborate. Instead of seeing differences, we should embrace the beauty of unity.

Rather than pushing people away, we should welcome them. ***A strong community is one where people feel accepted regardless of their flaws.*** We all struggle, but together, we can overcome challenges with love and support. Judging others only creates division, but encouragement builds bridges. **Romans 15:7** says, *"Accept one another, then, just as Christ accepted you, in order to bring praise to God."* Inclusion creates belonging, and when we open our hearts, we create a space where people feel safe.

A community is not just about gathering—it is about deep connection. Friendship, family, and faith are strengthened when people work together, care for one another, and listen with compassion. Instead of focusing on what separates us, we should focus on what unites us. **Ecclesiastes 4:9-10** says, *"Two are better than one... If either of them falls down, one can help the other up."* This verse reminds us that we complete each other, and the best way to grow is through support and kindness.

When we build strong communities, we create a world where love and unity thrive. When we recognize that no one is better than the other, and that we all need help at different times, we create an environment of trust and care. **Galatians 6:2** tells us, *"Carry each other's burdens, and in this way, you will fulfill the law of Christ."* Life is not about standing alone—it is about standing together, supporting, forgiving, and growing in love.

SYAVIHA MULENGYA

4. Care

Care is one of the most powerful expressions of love. It means looking after others, offering support, and showing concern for their well-being. When we care for others, we remind them that they are valued, important, and not alone. **Philippians 2:4** says, *"Let each of you look not only to his own interests, but also to the interests of others."* This verse teaches us that life should not be selfish—we must also think about the needs of those around us.

Caring for others is more than words—it is action. Many people say they care, but they do not show it. True care is demonstrated through kindness, patience, and selflessness. When we take time to listen, offer a helping hand, or simply be present for someone in need, we make a difference. **Galatians 6:2** reminds us, *"Carry each other's burdens, and in this way, you will fulfill the law of Christ."* This means that we should help others in their struggles, just as we hope they will help us in ours.

Care is a cycle—it spreads from one person to another. The more we practice it, the more it grows. Sometimes, caring for others requires sacrifice, but love is always worth it. **Romans 12:10** says, *"Be devoted to one another in love. Honor one another above yourselves."* When we sincerely care for others, we create a world filled with kindness, connection, and understanding.

5. Complement

We complete each other. No one is meant to do everything alone or be perfect in all things. Each person has different strengths and abilities, and together, we balance each other. **Ecclesiastes 4:9-10** says, *"Two are better than one... If either of them falls down, one can help the other up."* This verse reminds us that we need one another to succeed, grow, and overcome challenges.

SYAVIHA MULENGYA

Instead of competing, we should complement each other. Some people are leaders, while others are great supporters. Some excel in thinking, while others are skilled in action. When we work together, we create something beautiful. **1 Corinthians 12:12** tells us, *"For just as the body is one and has many members, and all the members of the body, though many, are one body, so it is with Christ."* This means that every person has a role, and each role is important in life.

Complementing each other also means appreciating differences. We should not judge others for being different. Instead, we should celebrate their uniqueness. Every person has something valuable to offer, and when we accept this, we create a world where everyone feels loved, accepted, and appreciated.

6. Consideration

Consideration means being mindful of others—thinking about their feelings, needs, and struggles before taking action. It means treating people with kindness and respect. **Philippians 2:3** says, *"Do nothing out of selfish ambition or vain conceit. Rather, in humility value others above yourselves."* This verse reminds us that life is not about proving we are better—it is about showing love and humility.

Often, people act without considering how their actions affect others. Harsh words, selfish decisions, and a lack of empathy can deeply hurt people. But true wisdom comes from being considerate. **Ephesians 4:32** says, *"Be kind to one another, tenderhearted, forgiving one another, as God in Christ forgave you."* This teaches us that kindness should guide our choices and interactions with others.

Consideration creates a world where people feel safe and valued. When we choose patience over anger and kindness over judgment, we bring healing instead of harm. Instead of ignoring the needs of those around us, we should reach out and offer support. True strength is found in love, and when we practice consideration, we make life better for everyone.

7. Celebration

Life is precious, and every moment deserves to be appreciated. Every person is valuable, and their journey should be recognized with kindness and joy. There is no reason for us to fight, to compare, or to tear each other down. Instead, we should lift, love, and care for one another. **Psalm 118:24** tells us, "*This is the day that the Lord has made; let us rejoice and be glad in it.*" Each day is a gift—an opportunity to spread peace, encouragement, and positivity. When we celebrate life, we shift our focus from negativity to gratitude, reminding ourselves that there is always something to be thankful for.

Celebration is more than parties and events—it is a way of life. It means appreciating friendships, valuing relationships, and seeing the beauty in simple moments. Many people focus on their struggles and forget to recognize their victories, even the small ones. But every achievement, every step forward, and every moment of kindness deserves acknowledgment. **1 Thessalonians 5:16-18** encourages us, "*Rejoice always, pray continually, give thanks in all circumstances.*" A heart filled with gratitude sees blessings even in difficulties, and true joy comes from appreciating both the good and the challenging moments.

Celebrating others is just as important as celebrating ourselves. Instead of competing with people, we should support them. Instead of feeling jealous, we should be happy for their success. Encouragement can uplift someone who is struggling and remind them that they are not alone. When we take time to appreciate

SYAVIHA MULENGYA

those around us, we build strong connections. **Romans 12:10** says, *"Be devoted to one another in love. Honor one another above yourselves."* This verse teaches that true celebration is rooted in love—it is about recognizing the value in every person and choosing to uplift rather than tear down.

When we embrace celebration, we create a culture of joy and unity. A world filled with appreciation and kindness is a world where love thrives. ***Instead of focusing on what is lacking, we should focus on what is abundant.*** Whether big or small, moments of celebration bring hope, healing, and happiness. **Galatians 6:9** reminds us, *"Let us not grow weary in doing good, for at the proper time we will reap a harvest if we do not give up."* When we consistently encourage and uplift others, we build a life filled with meaning and purpose.

Celebration is a choice. It is the decision to see the good in people, to embrace gratitude, and to create a space where everyone feels valued. We are one, and we need each other. Instead of dividing, we should unite. Instead of judging, we should love. **Ecclesiastes 4:9** reminds us, *"Two are better than one because they have a good return for their labor."* The more we celebrate and lift each other up, the stronger and more beautiful our world becomes.

8. Connection

Connection is what brings people together. It is about building relationships, supporting one another, and knowing that we are never alone. **Hebrews 10:24-25** says, *"And let us consider how we may spur one another on toward love and good deeds, not giving up meeting together, but encouraging one another."* This verse reminds us that we need each other to grow, to love, and to live fully.

Often, people feel isolated, believing they must face life's challenges alone. But connection reminds us that we are stronger together. When we support one another, we create a world where no one feels abandoned. **Acts 2:44-45** says, *"All the believers were together and had everything in common. They sold property and possessions to give to anyone who had need."* **This shows that true connection is about sharing, helping, and standing by each other.**

Instead of pushing people away, we should welcome them in. Instead of judging, we should encourage. Connection is not just about being in the same place—it is about being united in heart and purpose. When we build strong connections, we create a world where love and unity thrive.

SYAVIHA MULENGYA

5

*** *** ***

HONOR EVERY PERSON

Mirembe was a beautiful woman. She walked with confidence, dressed in the finest clothes, and carried herself like a queen. Many admired her, and many men approached her with love. But each time, she would say, "You are not my class." She believed she deserved someone more successful, more important, someone who matched her high standards. She refused any man who did not meet her perfect image.

As the years passed, Mirembe remained unmarried. The men she had rejected had moved on, built families, and found happiness. But she was alone. She had spent so much time thinking she was better than others that she had lost the chance to build meaningful relationships. Not only did she reject love, but she also turned down career opportunities. She refused jobs, saying they were not good enough for her. She thought something better would always come—but it never did.

Her once busy life became quiet. The people who had admired her slowly drifted away. She had spent years looking down on others, never realizing that she needed them. **Proverbs 16:18** says, *"Pride goes before destruction, a haughty spirit before a fall."*

SYAVIHA MULENGYA

Mirembe's pride had cost her everything. She had believed she was above others, but now, she was left with nothing.

One day, she sat alone, thinking about the choices she had made. She realized how much she had missed by neglecting others. Love, friendship, and happiness had been within her reach, but she had let them slip away. **James 4:6** says, "*God opposes the proud but shows favor to the humble.*" She finally understood that true beauty is found in kindness, humility, and appreciation for others.

Mirembe's story teaches us a powerful lesson—no one is better than another. We all need love, respect, and care. Neglecting people leads to loneliness, regret, and missed opportunities. Life is not about standing above others—it is about standing together. **Galatians 6:2** reminds us, "*Carry each other's burdens, and in this way, you will fulfill the law of Christ.*" The greatest joy comes not from pride but from loving and uplifting those around us

Neglecting others can lead to division, isolation, and missed opportunities for growth. We are meant to support, love, and care for one another, not to judge or ignore those in need. **Matthew 7:1-2** warns, "*Do not judge, or you too will be judged. For in the same way you judge others, you will be judged.*" This verse reminds us that looking down on others can bring consequences. Instead of neglecting people, we should embrace kindness, humility, and understanding.

When we fail to acknowledge others' struggles, we limit ourselves. We miss the chance to learn from different perspectives, to grow in wisdom, and to build meaningful relationships. **Proverbs 14:21** says, "*Whoever despises his neighbor is a sinner, but blessed is he who is generous to the poor.*" This verse teaches that neglecting others is not only harmful to them but also to ourselves. True wisdom is shown through compassion, not superiority.

SYAVIHA MULENGYA

Neglecting others also leads to a lack of empathy. When we stop caring about people's feelings and experiences, we become cold and disconnected. **James 4:11-12** reminds us, *"Do not slander one another. Anyone who speaks against a brother or sister or judges them speaks against the law."* This verse encourages us to treat others with respect and dignity, recognizing that we all have struggles.

Ignoring people can also cause us to lose blessings. **Galatians 5:13-14** says, *"Serve one another humbly in love. For the entire law is fulfilled in keeping this one command: 'Love your neighbor as yourself.'"* When we neglect others, we miss the opportunity to experience the joy of giving, helping, and building strong connections.

The Danger of Neglecting Others

1. Looking Down on People

Looking down on others creates division and destroys relationships. It builds walls where God calls us to build bridges. No one is better than another—we all carry strengths and weaknesses, victories and wounds. **Proverbs 16:18** warns, *"Pride goes before destruction, a haughty spirit before a fall."* **Arrogance may feel powerful, but it leads to isolation and downfall. When we judge others by their status, skin, or story, we miss the heart of Christ**. He didn't come to elevate the elite—He came to embrace the overlooked. Humility and kindness are not just virtues; they are healing agents. They restore what pride ruins. When we choose to honor instead of compare, we reflect the kingdom of God. Every person matters. Every soul deserves dignity.

Seeing ourselves as superior blinds us to the beauty in others. It blocks growth, connection, and compassion. **Romans 12:3** urges us, *"Do not think of yourself more highly than you ought, but rather think of yourself with sober judgment."* That's not self-hate—it's spiritual clarity. True wisdom sees worth in every person, not just the polished or powerful. When we dismiss others, we dismiss the gifts God placed in them. Looking down damages trust and erodes respect. People feel unseen, unheard, and unloved. **James 2:1** reminds us, *"Believers in our glorious Lord Jesus Christ must not show favoritism."* That means no more ranking people—only reaching people. **Let's choose fairness over favoritism, dignity over division, and grace over pride.** Who have you overlooked, and how can you honor them today?

2. Limiting Ourselves

When we neglect others, we limit our own potential. God designed us to grow through connection, not isolation. Every person we meet carries a unique perspective, a lesson, and a reflection of God's creativity. When we choose to ignore or dismiss others, we miss the sharpening that comes through relationships. **Proverbs 27:17** says, *"As iron sharpens iron, so one person sharpens another."* This verse reminds us that growth is mutual—we are refined, challenged, and strengthened through others. Neglect is not just a lack of attention; it's a missed opportunity for transformation. When we engage with others, we expand our understanding, deepen our compassion, and stretch our faith. The people around us are not obstacles—they are mirrors, mentors, and messengers. To neglect them is to neglect the tools God uses to shape us.

Isolation may feel safe, but it leads to stagnation. When we pull away from others, we stop learning. We stop listening. We stop growing. **Ecclesiastes 4:9** says, *"Two are better than one because they have a good return for their labor."* This truth reveals that partnership multiplies impact. Alone, we may survive—but together, we thrive. God never intended for us to walk alone. Even Jesus surrounded Himself with disciples, friends, and community. When we isolate, we lose the strength that comes from shared burdens and shared victories. We become vulnerable to pride, fear, and spiritual dryness. Growth requires friction, and friction requires fellowship. To flourish, we must be willing to connect, collaborate, and be sharpened.

Neglecting others also robs us of life's richness. Every person carries a story worth hearing, a gift worth receiving, and a lesson worth learning. When we close ourselves off, we miss the beauty of human connection. We miss the laughter, the wisdom, the healing that comes through shared experience. God often speaks through people—through their testimonies, their kindness, their presence. When we neglect others, we silence voices that were meant to bless us. We miss divine appointments. We miss the chance to be a blessing in return. True joy is found not in isolation, but in interaction. To recognize the value in others is to recognize the heart of God. When we honor people, we honor the One who made them. **Romans 15:7** says, *"Accept one another, then, just as Christ accepted you."* True fulfillment comes from embracing others, not rejecting them.

3. Lack of Empathy

Empathy is the ability to understand and share others' feelings. When we neglect people, we lose this important quality. **Ephesians 4:32** says, *"Be kind and compassionate to one another, forgiving each other, just as in Christ God forgave you."* Without empathy, relationships suffer, and people feel isolated.

A lack of empathy leads to misunderstanding and conflict. When we fail to recognize others' struggles, we become judgmental and harsh. **Colossians 3:12** reminds us, *"Clothe yourselves with compassion, kindness, humility, gentleness, and patience."* These qualities strengthen relationships and bring peace.

Neglecting empathy also makes us indifferent to suffering. Instead of helping, we turn away. **Luke 6:36** says, "Be merciful, just as your Father is merciful." True strength is found in kindness, not in ignoring those in need.

4. Losing Our Blessings

When we neglect others, we miss the blessings that come from kindness and generosity. **Proverbs 11:25** says, *"A generous person will prosper; whoever refreshes others will be refreshed."* Helping others brings joy and fulfillment.

Neglecting people leads to missed opportunities. Many times, blessings come through relationships, support, and shared wisdom. **Galatians 6:9** reminds us, *"Let us not grow weary in doing good, for at the proper time we will reap a harvest if we do not give up."* When we care for others, we receive blessings in return.

True happiness comes from giving, not withholding. **Acts 20:35** says, *"It is more blessed to give than to receive."* When we neglect others, we deny ourselves the joy of making a difference.

5. Lies

Neglecting others can lead to dishonesty. When we ignore people, we may justify our actions with excuses or false beliefs. **Proverbs 12:22** says, *"The Lord detests lying lips, but he delights in people who are trustworthy."* Truth and integrity strengthen relationships.

SYAVIHA MULENGYA

Lies create division and mistrust. When we deceive others, we damage connections and lose respect. **Ephesians 4:25** reminds us, *"Each of you must put off falsehood and speak truthfully to your neighbor."* Honesty builds strong relationships. Neglecting people often leads to self-deception. We convince ourselves that we do not need others, but the truth is, we do. **John 8:32** says, *"Then you will know the truth, and the truth will set you free."* Facing reality allows us to grow and heal.

6. Lament

Neglecting others can lead to regret. Many people realize too late that they should have been more caring. **Psalm 34:18** says, *"The Lord is close to the brokenhearted and saves those who are crushed in spirit."* Ignoring people can cause deep sorrow.

Lament comes when we recognize missed opportunities. When we fail to show kindness, we may later wish we had done more. **2 Corinthians 7:10** reminds us, *"Godly sorrow brings repentance that leads to salvation and leaves no regret."* Learning from mistakes helps us grow. Instead of waiting until it is too late, we should choose love now. **Romans 12:15** says, *"Rejoice with those who rejoice; mourn with those who mourn."* Being present for others brings healing and connection.

7. Loneliness

Neglecting others leads to isolation. ***When we push people away, we create loneliness for ourselves and for them***. **Proverbs 18:1** warns, *"Whoever isolates himself seeks his own desire; he breaks out against all sound judgment."* Connection is essential for a fulfilling life.

Loneliness affects emotional and mental well-being. People need companionship, encouragement, and love. **Genesis 2:18** says, *"It is not good for man to be alone."* We are designed for relationships, and neglecting them leads to emptiness.

Instead of neglecting people, we should build strong connections. **Hebrews 13:1** reminds us, *"Keep on loving one another as brothers and sisters."* Love brings people together, creating a world where no one feels forgotten.

6

******

THE DANGERS OF RACISM AND TRIBALISM

Racism and tribalism are not just social issues—they are spiritual poisons that infect hearts, divide communities, and dishonor God's design for humanity. These evils creep in quietly, often disguised as pride, tradition, or loyalty, but their fruit is always bitter. They teach us to judge others by skin color, language, or lineage rather than by character, kindness, and calling. When we allow these poisons to shape our thinking, we lose sight of the truth that every person is made in the image of God. The result is division, where unity should thrive; suspicion, where trust should grow; and hatred, where love should reign. **Galatians 3:28** reminds us that in Christ, there is no Jew or Gentile, slave or free— we are all one. That unity is not just a theological idea; it's a divine command. Racism and tribalism fight against this truth, replacing grace with judgment and fellowship with fear. They rob us of the joy of diversity and the strength of shared purpose. If we are to reflect God's heart, we must completely reject these poisons. We must choose love, justice, and unity.

The damage caused by racism and tribalism is deep and far-reaching. It breaks families, weakens churches, and destabilizes

SYAVIHA MULENGYA

nations. It creates systems of exclusion where only a few are allowed to rise, while others are pushed down and forgotten. This leads to inequality in education, employment, leadership, and opportunity. It silences voices that were meant to speak life and wisdom. It causes people to doubt their worth and question their place in the world. But God's Word tells us that we are fearfully and wonderfully made, each with a unique purpose. When we discriminate, we deny that truth and block the blessings that come from diversity. Tribalism teaches us to protect our own at the expense of others, but love teaches us to serve all. Racism teaches us to fear what is different, but faith teaches us to embrace it. Healing begins when we stop defending division and start defending dignity.

From Division to God's Vision

Racism and tribalism also poison our witness as believers. When the church reflects the world's divisions, it loses its power to transform. We cannot preach love while practicing exclusion. We cannot sing of grace while showing favoritism. The gospel is for every tribe, tongue, and nation—not just for those who look or speak like us. Jesus broke barriers everywhere He went—touching lepers, dining with sinners, and honoring Samaritans. His life was a protest against prejudice and a model of radical inclusion. If we claim to follow Him, we must walk the same path. That means confronting bias in our hearts, our homes, and our institutions. It means creating spaces where everyone is welcomed, valued, and empowered. The world is watching, and our love must be louder than its hate.

*To reject the poison of racism and tribalism, we must be intentional and brave. **It starts with teaching our children to love beyond borders. Every culture holds beauty, and every person***

SYAVIHA MULENGYA

carries worth. *We must challenge harmful ideas and replace lies with truth.* Stereotypes must be broken through honest conversations. Instead of staying in our comfort zones, we should reach out and build real connections. Relationships across race and tribe help us grow in understanding. Listening to different stories opens our hearts and minds. We must admit where we've failed and choose to forgive those who've hurt us. This work is not easy, but it is sacred. God calls us to be part of healing what hate has tried to destroy.

This journey requires humility and strength. **We must be willing to change and let God shape our hearts.** Love is stronger than fear, and grace is deeper than division. When we choose kindness, we reflect God's heart. *"Blessed are the peacemakers, for they will be called children of God."* — **Matthew 5:9.** We are called to be bridge-builders, not wall-builders. Peacemakers bring light into dark places. Truth-tellers speak with love and courage. Forgiveness opens the door to restoration. Unity begins when we see each other as family. Together, we can rebuild what prejudice has torn apart.

God's love reaches beyond every border. His grace embraces every tribe, language, and nation. Each person is made in His image, carrying equal worth and divine purpose. *"There is neither Jew nor Gentile... for you are all one in Christ Jesus."* — **Galatians 3:28.** With this truth, we rise in hope and walk in compassion. Speak out when injustice appears. Stand beside those who have been wounded or overlooked. Build communities that honor diversity and unity. Speak truth with courage and live it with conviction. This is sacred work—work that reflects the heart of God. Together, we shine with grace, justice, and love.

SYAVIHA MULENGYA

Danger Of Racism and Tribalism

One Body, One Family, No Divisions

1. Division

Racism and tribalism divide people who were created to live in unity. They build invisible walls that separate hearts, families, and communities. These walls are made of fear, pride, and misunderstanding. When we focus only on differences, we forget the beauty of diversity. God designed us to complement each other, not compete. **Galatians 3:28** reminds us that we are one in Christ, not separated by race or status. Division weakens the bonds that hold society together. It turns neighbors into strangers and friends into enemies. Instead of working together, we pull apart and lose strength. Jesus prayed that we would be united, just as He is with the Father. That unity is not optional—it is God's desire for His people.

Division also affects how we see ourselves and others. It creates a mindset of superiority and inferiority. People begin to believe lies about their worth based on where they come from. This leads to broken identities and wounded spirits. Families suffer when members are taught to distrust others. Communities lose their power when they are split by hate. Nations crumble when unity is replaced by tribal pride. God calls us to live in peace and harmony. We are meant to celebrate our differences, not fear them. Every culture has something beautiful to offer. When we divide, we miss the gifts others bring.

The devil uses division to distract us from God's purpose. He wants us to fight each other instead of fighting for each other. Division is a tool of destruction, not growth. It keeps us from building strong relationships. It blocks progress and delays healing.

SYAVIHA MULENGYA

When we are divided, we cannot stand together in times of trouble. We lose the ability to support and uplift one another. God's plan is for unity, not separation. We must reject the lies that cause division. We must choose love over fear. Unity is strength, and strength brings victory.

Healing division starts with a change of heart. We must be willing to listen, learn, and love. We must see others as God sees them—equal and valuable. It takes courage to cross the lines that divide us. But every step toward unity is a step toward peace. We can build bridges where walls once stood. We can speak words that heal instead of hurt. We can choose kindness over judgment. God is calling us to be peacemakers. Let's answer that call with boldness and grace. Let's be the generation that chooses unity.

To overcome division, we must act with intention and faith. We must forgive past hurts and seek reconciliation. We must invite others into our lives and learn from their stories. We must stop judging and start understanding. We must pray for healing in our families and communities. We must teach unity in our homes and churches. We must celebrate the beauty of every tribe and race. We must stand together in love and truth. God's love is bigger than our differences. His grace is stronger than our fears. Let's walk together in unity and reflect His heart.

2. Discrimination: Hurting Hearts and Blocking Blessings

Discrimination is a silent destroyer of dreams. It tells people they are not good enough because of their race or tribe. It shuts doors that God meant to be open. It creates pain that is often hidden but deeply felt. **James 2:9** says that showing favoritism is sin. When we treat people unfairly, we go against God's law of love. *Discrimination makes people feel invisible and unwanted.* It robs them of dignity and hope. It limits their potential and crushes their spirit. God created every person with purpose and value. No one should be judged by the color of their skin or the tribe they belong to.

Discrimination also damages the heart of the one who discriminates. It blinds them to the beauty in others. It makes them cold, proud, and distant. They miss out on friendships, wisdom, and growth. Prejudice is a prison that keeps people from loving freely. It creates fear and feeds ignorance. God wants us to love without limits. He wants us to see others through His eyes. Every person is a reflection of His image. When we discriminate, we dishonor that image. We must choose to love beyond labels.

Discrimination leaves deep wounds—in schools, workplaces, and even places of worship. It denies people the dignity they deserve and keeps them from reaching their full potential. It divides communities that were meant to thrive in unity. But God's kingdom is built on justice and mercy. As His people, we are called to speak up for those who cannot speak for themselves, to stand beside the marginalized, and to act with courage and compassion. *"Learn to do right; seek justice. Defend the oppressed."* — **Isaiah 1:17**

Love is the force that breaks down walls. When we choose fairness and kindness, we reflect the heart of God. *"There is neither Jew nor Gentile, neither slave nor free, nor is there male and female, for you are all one in Christ Jesus."* — **Galatians 3:28**. Let's be people who lift others up, who build bridges instead of barriers, and who live out the radical love of Christ.

Healing begins with humility—with repentance and a desire to be transformed. We must acknowledge where we've gone wrong and ask God to renew our hearts. *"If my people, who are called by my name, will humble themselves and pray and seek my face... then*

I will hear from heaven… and will heal their land." — **2 Chronicles 7:14**

Listening deeply, creating inclusive spaces, and teaching our children to love without prejudice are steps toward restoration. God's love knows no boundaries. His grace reaches every tribe and tongue. *"Above all, love each other deeply, because love covers over a multitude of sins."* — **1 Peter 4:8.** Let's be vessels of that grace— champions of kindness, humility, and equality.

To defeat discrimination, we must live intentionally. We must speak out against injustice, support those who've been wounded, and challenge systems that perpetuate inequality. *"Speak up for those who cannot speak for themselves… defend the rights of the poor and needy."* — **Proverbs 31:8-9**

Building friendships across cultures and celebrating the gifts others bring reflects the beauty of God's diverse creation. Let our lives be living testimonies of His love—bold in truth, rich in mercy. *"You are the light of the world. A city set on a hill cannot be hidden."* — **Matthew 5:14**. Through prayer, action, and unity, we can shine light into dark places. Let's be the hands and feet of Jesus—bringing justice, mercy, and hope wherever we go.

3. Dehumanization: Forgetting the Image of God

Dehumanization is one of the most dangerous effects of racism and tribalism. It happens when people stop seeing others as human beings with value and dignity. Instead, they see them as problems, threats, or objects to be controlled. This mindset leads to cruelty, injustice, and deep emotional harm. **Genesis 1:27** tells us that every person is made in the image of God. That means every life carries divine worth, no matter their background. When we dehumanize others, we insult the Creator who made them. We strip away the respect that every person deserves. We open the door to violence, rejection, and oppression. History has shown us how this thinking leads to slavery, genocide, and war. It begins with a thought, but it ends in tragedy.

Dehumanization also affects how we treat people in everyday life. It shows up in how we speak, how we act, and how we make decisions. When we ignore someone's pain or dismiss their voice, we are denying their humanity. When we stereotype or mock others, we are feeding the poison of hate. Jesus never treated anyone as less than human. He touched the sick, welcomed the outcast, and honored the broken. His love was full of compassion and respect. He saw people not for their flaws, but for their potential. We are called to follow His example in how we treat others. Every person we meet is someone God loves deeply. We must choose to see them through His eyes.

The damage of dehumanization goes beyond the moment—it leaves lasting scars. People who are treated as less than human often carry deep wounds. They feel invisible, unwanted, and unloved. This pain can affect their confidence, their relationships, and their future. It can also create anger, bitterness, and fear. But healing is possible when we choose love over hate. When we speak life and show kindness, we help restore what was broken. We become agents of healing in a hurting world. God wants us to lift others up, not tear them down. We must be voices of hope and hands of mercy. Let's be people who honor the image of God in everyone.

To fight dehumanization, we must start with our hearts. We must ask God to remove pride, prejudice, and fear. We must learn to listen, understand, and care. We must teach others to value every life. We must speak out when we see injustice. We must

SYAVIHA MULENGYA

create spaces where everyone feels safe and respected. We must remember that love is stronger than hate. Compassion is more powerful than cruelty. Respect builds bridges, while hate builds walls. Let's be known for how we love, not how we judge. Let's reflect the heart of Jesus in every interaction.

4. Denial

Denial is another painful result of racism and tribalism. It happens when people are denied opportunities, rights, and respect because of who they are. It's not always loud—it can be quiet and hidden. But its effects are deep and lasting. **Proverbs 18:13** warns us against answering before listening. When we refuse to hear someone's story, we deny their humanity. We ignore their pain and silence their voice. Denial keeps people from growing and thriving. It blocks access to education, jobs, and justice. It creates systems that favor some and exclude others. This is not God's way.

God is a God of justice, mercy, and truth. He wants every person to be treated fairly and with love. Denial goes against everything He stands for. It is rooted in pride, fear, and ignorance. It causes people to feel rejected and forgotten. It keeps communities stuck in cycles of poverty and pain. It stops progress and breaks trust. When we deny someone's worth, we deny the work of God in their life. We must choose to open doors, not close them. We must choose to include, not exclude. Every person deserves a chance to shine.

Denial affects how we treat others and build relationships. It creates space between people and makes it harder to build trust. When someone feels ignored or left out, they may feel lonely, sad, or even angry. This kind of hurt can grow over time and damage hearts. But God wants us to be people who welcome others with love. He asks us to make places where everyone feels noticed and valued. We need to include others on purpose, not by accident. Showing kindness can change someone's day. Our words should help, not harm. In a world that often shuts people out, we can be the hands and feet of Jesus. *"Accept one another, then, just as Christ accepted you."* — **Romans 15:7**

To overcome denial, we must take real steps. We should listen to those who feel unheard. We need to speak up for people who have been pushed aside. It's important to challenge unfair systems and ideas. Let's build communities that show God's love to everyone. We can teach others to see the value in every person. Love should be strong, and kindness should be bold. Every person has a story worth hearing. Every life matters and has purpose. Let's open doors, not close them. *"Do not merely listen to the word... Do what it says."* — **James 1:22**

5. Damage

Racism and tribalism cause deep and lasting damage. They hurt individuals, families, and entire communities. The pain is not just emotional—it affects every part of life. **Proverbs 14:31** says that oppressing the poor shows contempt for their Maker. When we harm others because of their race or tribe, we dishonor God. The damage includes broken trust, lost opportunities, and shattered dreams. It creates fear, anger, and division. It stops people from reaching their full potential. It keeps communities from growing and thriving. It leaves scars that can last for generations. This is not what God wants for His children.

The damage also affects how people see themselves. They begin to believe the lies told about them. They lose confidence and hope. They feel unwanted and unloved. This can lead to depression, isolation, and despair. But God speaks truth over every life. He says

SYAVIHA MULENGYA

we are fearfully and wonderfully made. He says we are chosen, loved, and called. His truth heals what hate has broken. His love restores what pain has stolen. We must speak that truth into every hurting heart.

Communities damaged by racism and tribalism need healing. They need leaders who will stand for justice and peace. They need people who will build bridges, not walls. They need churches that welcome everyone. They need schools that teach love and respect. They need workplaces that value every voice. Healing takes time, but it starts with love. It grows through kindness, fairness, and courage. God is calling us to be healers. He wants us to repair what has been torn apart. Let's answer that call with boldness.

To heal the damage, we must be honest and humble. We must admit where we've failed. We must ask God to guide us in love. We must forgive and seek forgiveness. We must choose unity over division. We must choose grace over judgment. We must choose peace over pride. Healing is possible when we walk in God's truth. It begins with one act of love, one word of hope, one step of faith. Let's be part of the healing. Let's bring light where there has been darkness.

6. Dishonor: Rejecting God's Design

Racism and tribalism go against the image of God in every person. When we treat someone as less because of their race or tribe, we dishonor the One who created them. God made each person with care, purpose, and dignity. Judging by appearance causes us to forget that truth. This dishonor shows up in what we say, how we act, and even when we stay silent. *"Whoever mocks the poor shows contempt for their Maker."* — **Proverbs 17:5**. That disrespect is not just toward people—it's toward God Himself.

SYAVIHA MULENGYA

Dishonor breaks trust and brings shame. It makes people hide instead of celebrating who they are. It distorts how we see others and ourselves. God calls us to honor everyone, because each life reflects His glory.

Dishonor also weakens the respect that holds communities together. When we fail to value others, we create fear and rejection. People stop sharing their gifts because they feel unwanted. Dreams fade when people feel unworthy. Voices meant to bring life are silenced. Dishonor pushes people aside and keeps them from growing. But God's kingdom is built on love and honor. Jesus welcomed the poor, the sick, and the outcast. He saw worth where others saw shame. We are called to do the same—in our homes, churches, and workplaces. *"Show proper respect to everyone, love the family of believers."* — **1 Peter 2:17**. Honor brings healing where dishonor has caused pain.

Dishonor also affects how we worship and serve. When prejudice lives in our hearts, it blocks love from flowing freely. It divides the body of Christ and weakens our witness to the world. God wants His people to be known for love, not bias. He calls us to lift others up, not tear them down. Dishonor makes us forget we belong to one body. It leads to competition instead of unity. It stirs up jealousy, pride, and conflict. But choosing honor brings peace and growth. It opens the door to grace and healing. *"Be devoted to one another in love. Honor one another above yourselves."* — **Romans 12:10**. Let's be people who honor others in every part of life.

To overcome dishonor, we must begin with humility. We need to see the value in every person we meet. Our words should build up, not break down. We should celebrate the strengths of others, even when they're different from ours. Honor starts at home and spreads through our communities. We must ask God to remove pride and prejudice from our hearts. Seeing others through love changes everything. Honor is more than a feeling—it's a choice. It's a way of living that shows God's heart. Let's be known for how we lift others, not how we judge. *"Therefore encourage one another and build each other up."* — **1 Thessalonians 5:11.** Let's restore dignity where it's been lost.

7. Discouragement: Stealing Strength and Hope

Racism and tribalism create deep discouragement in the hearts of those affected. They send the message that some people will never be good enough. This message crushes dreams and weakens confidence. It makes people question their worth and doubt their future. Discouragement is a heavy burden that many carry silently. It affects how people think, speak, and act. It keeps them from trying, from hoping, and from believing. God never intended for His children to live under such a weight. He speaks life, not defeat. **Isaiah 41:10** says, *"Do not fear, for I am with you… I will strengthen you and help you."* That promise is for everyone, no matter their background.

Discouragement also affects how people relate to others. When someone feels rejected, they often pull away. They stop trusting, stop sharing, and stop connecting. This creates loneliness and isolation. It breaks the bonds that were meant to bring healing. Racism and tribalism feed this cycle by creating constant reminders of exclusion. But God's love breaks through discouragement. His Word lifts the weary and restores the broken. We must be people who speak encouragement, not criticism. We must remind others of their value and potential. Encouragement is a gift we can give every day.

Discouragement can also affect entire communities. When people are constantly told they don't belong, they stop building. They stop dreaming of better schools, safer streets, and stronger families. They settle for less because they've been told they deserve less. This is a lie from the enemy, not the truth of God. God wants communities to thrive, not just survive. He wants leaders to rise, children to dream, and families to flourish. We must break the cycle of discouragement with words of hope and acts of love. We must create spaces where people feel seen and supported. Let's be builders of courage in places where fear has ruled.

To overcome discouragement, we must become encouragers. We must speak life into those who feel defeated. We must remind them of God's promises and their purpose. We must celebrate small victories and offer help in hard times. We must be present, patient, and persistent. Encouragement is not just about words— it's about presence. It's about showing up and standing with others. God uses encouragers to heal hearts and restore hope. Let's be those people in our families, churches, and communities. Let's replace discouragement with strength and joy. Let's be the light that lifts others up.

8. Despair: The Darkness That Tries to Win

Despair is one of the deepest wounds caused by racism and tribalism. It brings the feeling that nothing will ever improve. It whispers that no one sees, no one cares, and no one will help. This kind of pain leads people to give up—on themselves and on others. Sadness, isolation, and even self-harm often follow. But this is not the life God desires for His children. *"The Lord is close to the brokenhearted and saves those who are crushed in spirit."* — **Psalm 34:18**. Every tear is seen, every cry is heard. God stays near to those who feel forgotten. Despair may shout loudly, but His love speaks louder. Light still shines in the darkest places.

Hopelessness also changes how people view their future. Dreams fade, and plans are abandoned. Success begins to feel out of reach. A heavy cloud blocks vision and purpose. Yet God restores what was lost and brings new hope. Every person is loved, chosen, and capable. Rising is possible, even after falling. Despair tells lies, but truth brings freedom. Voices of encouragement must speak boldly. Every story is still unfolding—God is not finished. Beautiful chapters are still being written.

When one person loses hope, the impact can the families and communities. Children may grow up feeling limited. Parents may stop believing change is possible. Leaders may lose the courage to guide. But despair is not the end. God can turn pain into purpose and build strength from brokenness. Hope must be carried into places of hurt. Light belongs in every corner. Love has the power to heal and restore. Hearts can believe again. Healing begins when hope is shared.

To overcome despair, real support must be present—not just in words, but in action. Listening with care brings comfort to those who feel unheard. Loving without limits reflects the heart of Christ, who never turned away the broken. Prayer opens the door to healing, and compassion brings peace to troubled souls. God's promises remind every person of their value and purpose. *"I have loved you with an everlasting love; I have drawn you with unfailing kindness."* — **Jeremiah 31:3**. Safe spaces allow people to grow, heal, and rediscover their strength. Gentle words can restore what pain has tried to silence. Faithful care and courageous love create lasting change. Despair loses its grip when hope stands firm. Light reaches the darkest places, and belief is born again—one heart at a time.

SYAVIHA MULENGYA

7

****

HOW TO WALK IN SOMEONE ELSE'S SHOES

Walking in Someone Else's Shoes

To walk in someone else's shoes is to step beyond your comfort and into compassion. It means choosing to see, feel, and understand life from another person's point of view. This journey is not about judgment—it's about grace. It's not about fixing others—it's about loving them. The Bible calls us to empathy, to kindness, and to humility. **Philippians 2:4** says, *"Let each of you look not only to his own interests, but also to the interests of others."* That is the heart of walking in someone else's shoes. It's a call to listen deeply, love boldly, and serve faithfully. When we walk with others, we reflect the love of Christ. We become bridges of healing, not walls of division. We become voices of hope, not echoes of criticism.

This kind of walk requires courage. It asks us to slow down, to ask questions, and to open our hearts. It's easy to stay in our own world, but love invites us to step into someone else's. Jesus did this every day—*He walked with the poor, the broken, the rejected. He didn't just preach from a distance; He touched lives up close.* He saw pain and responded with mercy. He saw confusion and answered with truth. He saw loneliness and offered friendship. That is our example. That is our calling. To walk in someone else's shoes is to walk like Jesus.

This journey also requires wisdom. It's not just about emotion—it's about intention. **Proverbs 4:7** says, *"Wisdom is the principal thing; therefore get wisdom."* When we walk with others, we must walk with discernment. We must learn to listen before we speak, to understand before we act. We must be willing to adapt, to accept, and to advocate. Each person's path is different, and love knows how to adjust. This walk is not always easy, but it is always worth it. It brings healing, unity, and transformation. It brings light into dark places. It brings peace where there was pain.

Walking in someone else's shoes is a ministry. It's a way to serve, to bless, and to build. **Galatians 6:2** says, *"Carry each other's burdens, and in this way you will fulfill the law of Christ."* That is the mission. That is the message. When we walk with others, we don't just change their lives—we change ours too. We grow in grace. We grow in love. We grow in understanding. This walk is not just a step—it's a lifestyle. It's a daily decision to love like Jesus. And when we do, we become the hands and feet of hope. Walking in someone else's shoes helps us build stronger relationships. It teaches us patience, kindness, and empathy. **Romans 15:7** says, "*Accept one another, then, just as Christ accepted you*." Instead of looking down on people, we should lift them up, support them, and show them they are valued.

1. Acknowledge

To walk in someone else's shoes, you must first acknowledge their existence, their experience, and their humanity. Many people are hurting, struggling, or silently enduring battles we cannot see. Acknowledging someone means seeing them—not just with your eyes, but with your heart. The Bible says in **Romans 12:15**, *"Rejoice with those who rejoice; mourn with those who mourn."* That verse invites us to step into the emotional world of others, not to fix it, but to feel it. When you acknowledge someone's pain, you validate their story. You say, "I see you, and you matter." This is the beginning of compassion. It's easy to ignore what we don't understand, but love calls us to lean in. Jesus acknowledged the blind man by the roadside, even though others told him to be quiet. He stopped, listened, and healed. That's the power of acknowledgment—it opens the door to healing.

Acknowledging someone also means recognizing their worth. Every person is made in the image of God, and that alone gives them value. **Genesis 1:27** reminds us that we are created in His likeness, which means no one is beneath our attention. When we acknowledge someone, we honor the Creator who made them. It's not about agreeing with everything they say or do—it's about respecting their journey. Sometimes people feel invisible, especially when they're different from us. But love doesn't discriminate. It sees beyond skin color, accent, background, or belief. Jesus acknowledged the Samaritan woman at the well, even though society rejected her. He spoke to her with dignity and truth. That moment changed her life and her village.

To acknowledge someone is to pause your own story and listen to theirs. It's a sacred act of humility. **Philippians 2:3** says, *"Do nothing out of selfish ambition or vain conceit. Rather, in humility value others above yourselves."* That doesn't mean you think less of yourself—it means you think of others more. When you acknowledge someone's pain, you don't minimize your own; you simply make room for theirs. This is how bridges are built. This is

SYAVIHA MULENGYA

how healing begins. You don't need to have all the answers. Just be present. Just say, "I see you." That simple act can restore hope.

Acknowledgment is also a form of worship. When you honor others, you honor God. **Proverbs 14:31** says, *"Whoever oppresses the poor shows contempt for their Maker, but whoever is kind to the needy honors Him."* Kindness begins with acknowledgment. It's the first step toward empathy. It's the first brick in the foundation of love. Don't rush past people. Don't assume their silence means peace. Look deeper. Ask God to give you eyes that see and a heart that feels. When you acknowledge someone, you become a vessel of grace

2. Ask Questions

Asking questions is a sacred invitation into someone's story. It shows that you care enough to understand, not just observe. **Proverbs 20:5** says, *"The purposes of a person's heart are deep waters, but one who has insight draws them out."* Questions are the tools of insight. They help us uncover the layers beneath someone's silence, smile, or sorrow. When you ask with sincerity, you build trust. You say, "I want to know you, not judge you." Jesus often asked questions—not because He didn't know the answers, but because He wanted people to reflect. "Who do you say I am?" He asked His disciples. That question still echoes today. Asking opens the door to a deeper connection.

Good questions are gentle, not invasive. They are rooted in love, not curiosity alone. **James 1:19** reminds us to be "quick to listen, slow to speak." That's the posture of someone who asks wisely. You don't need to interrogate—just invite. Ask about someone's dreams, their fears, their journey. Ask what brings them joy, what breaks their heart. These questions show that you value their voice. When you ask, you learn. And when you learn, you grow. Asking questions is not weakness—it's wisdom.

Jesus asked the man at the pool of Bethesda, *"Do you want to get well?"* (**John 5:6**). That question wasn't about physical healing alone—it was about readiness, desire, and hope. Sometimes the right question can stir something dormant in someone's soul. It can awaken purpose. It can ignite healing. When you ask, you give someone permission to speak. You give them space to be seen. You become a mirror reflecting their worth. Don't be afraid to ask. Just ask with love.

Asking questions also helps you avoid assumptions. It keeps your heart humble and your mind open. **Proverbs 18:13** warns, *"To answer before listening—that is folly and shame."* When you ask, you listen. And when you listen, you love. Questions are bridges. They connect hearts. They build empathy. They create understanding. So ask boldly, ask kindly, and ask often. You'll be amazed at what you discover.

3. Accept

Acceptance is not agreement—it's acknowledgment of someone's humanity. It's saying, "You belong, even if we're different." **Romans 15:7** says, *"Accept one another, then, just as Christ accepted you, in order to bring praise to God."* That kind of acceptance is radical. It's not based on performance, perfection, or similarity. It's based on grace. When you accept someone, you reflect the heart of Christ. You say, "You are worthy of love." Acceptance doesn't mean you condone every choice—it means you choose compassion over condemnation. Jesus accepted Zacchaeus before he changed. That acceptance led to transformation.

Acceptance is a powerful form of healing. Many people walk through life feeling rejected, unseen, or unworthy. Your acceptance can be a balm to their soul. It can restore dignity. It can rebuild trust. **Galatians 6:2** says, *"Carry each other's burdens, and in this way you will fulfill the law of Christ."* That begins with acceptance. You don't need to fix someone to love them. You just need to be present. Acceptance is the soil where grace grows.

Jesus accepted the woman caught in adultery when others wanted to stone her. He said, *"Neither do I condemn you. Go and sin no more."* (**John 8:11**). That moment was drenched in mercy. It was a turning point. Acceptance doesn't ignore truth—it delivers it with tenderness. When you accept someone, you create space for change. You become a safe place. You become a reflection of God's love. Acceptance is not passive—it's powerful.

To accept someone is to honor their journey. It's to say, "I may not understand everything, but I choose love." **1 Corinthians 13:7** says, *"Love bears all things, believes all things, hopes all things, endures all things."* That's the kind of love that transforms lives. Acceptance is not weakness—it's strength. It's the courage to love without conditions. It's the grace to embrace without judgment. *When you accept, you become a vessel of peace. You become a light in someone's darkness. You become a friend.*

4. Attend

To attend to someone is to be present—not just physically, but emotionally and spiritually. It means showing up with your heart open and your ears ready. **Luke 10:33-34** tells of the Good Samaritan who "came where the man was... took pity on him... bandaged his wounds." That's attending. It's active compassion. It's love in motion. Attending means you don't just notice pain—you respond to it. You don't just hear cries—you comfort them. You don't just see needs—you meet them. Attending is the ministry of presence.

When you attend to someone, you say, "You matter enough for me to pause." In a world that rushes, presence is a gift. It's a rare treasure. **Psalm 34:18** says, *"The Lord is close to the brokenhearted."* That's our model. God attends to us in our pain. He draws near. He listens. He comforts. When you attend to someone, you mirror that divine closeness. You become a channel of God's love.

Attending also means consistency. It's not a one-time act—it's a lifestyle. It's checking in, following up, staying close. It's remembering birthdays, noticing changes, and asking how someone's really doing. **Hebrews 10:24** says, *"Let us consider how we may spur one another on toward love and good deeds."* That requires attention. It requires care. *Attending is not glamorous, but it's glorious. It's the quiet work of love. To attend is to serve. It's to say, "I'm here for you." Jesus attended to the crowds, the sick, and the lonely. He never rushed past people. He stopped. He touched. He healed.* That's our example. When you attend to someone, you become the hands and feet of Christ. You become a living sermon. You become a blessing.

5. Adapt

Adaptation is the art of adjusting your heart, mind, and actions to meet someone where they are. It means letting go of rigid expectations and embracing flexibility for the sake of love. **Philippians 4:12** says, *"I know what it is to be in need, and I know what it is to have plenty... I have learned the secret of being content in any and every situation."* That's the spirit of adaptation—learning to be present in every season. When you adapt, you don't lose yourself; you expand yourself. You stretch your understanding, your

SYAVIHA MULENGYA

patience, and your grace. Jesus adapted to every person He met— He spoke to fishermen, tax collectors, and Pharisees with wisdom tailored to each heart. He didn't use one-size-fits-all love. He met people in their context. That's what love does—it bends without breaking. It listens before it leads.

Adaptation requires humility. It's the willingness to say, "I don't know everything, but I'm willing to learn." **Proverbs 3:5** reminds us to *"Trust in the Lord with all your heart and lean not on your own understanding."* That means letting go of pride and embracing curiosity. When you adapt, you become teachable. You stop demanding that others fit your mold. You start asking how you can serve them better. Adaptation is not compromise—it's compassion. It's the ability to shift your approach without losing your values. Jesus adapted His teaching style—sometimes He told stories, other times He asked questions. He knew that different hearts needed different doors. That's wisdom in action.

To adapt is to grow. It's to say, "I'm willing to change for the sake of connection." **Romans 12:2** says, *"Do not conform to the pattern of this world, but be transformed by the renewing of your mind."* That transformation includes how we relate to others. It means shedding assumptions and embracing empathy. Adaptation is not weakness—it's strength under control. It's the ability to pivot with purpose. When you adapt, you become more like Christ—who left heaven to walk among us. He adapted to our limitations so He could lift us higher. That's divine flexibility. That's love incarnate.

Adaptation also means being sensitive to timing. **Ecclesiastes 3:1** says, *"There is a time for everything, and a season for every activity under the heavens."* Some people need silence; others need words. Some need space; others need presence. Adapting means discerning what love looks like in each moment. It's not about doing more—it's about doing what matters. It's about listening to the Holy Spirit and responding with wisdom. When you adapt, you honor someone's journey. You say, "I'm not here to control you—I'm here to walk with you." That's the posture of grace. That's the rhythm of love.

6. Advocate

To advocate is to speak up for someone who may not have the strength or platform to speak for themselves. It's standing in the gap with courage and conviction. **Proverbs 31:8-9** says, *"Speak up for those who cannot speak for themselves... defend the rights of the poor and needy."* Advocacy is not just about words—it's about action. It's about using your influence to lift others. Jesus was the ultimate advocate—He defended the woman caught in adultery, He healed the leper, He welcomed the outcast. He didn't just preach love—He practiced it. Advocacy means you care enough to confront injustice. You care enough to challenge systems. You care enough to protect the vulnerable. That's love with a backbone.

Advocacy requires boldness. It's not always popular, but it's always powerful. Esther risked her life to advocate for her people, saying, *"If I perish, I perish."* (**Esther 4:16**). That's the heart of a true advocate—willing to sacrifice for the sake of others. When you advocate, you become a voice of hope. You become a shield for the weak. You become a light in dark places. Advocacy is not about being loud—it's about being clear. It's about speaking truth with love. It's about standing firm with grace. Jesus didn't back down from truth, but He always led with love.

To advocate is to intercede. It's to pray, to plead, to protect. **Romans 8:34** says, *"Christ Jesus... is at the right hand of God and is also interceding for us."* That's divine advocacy. When you pray for someone, you fight battles they may never see. You lift burdens they may never speak. You become a spiritual warrior. Advocacy is not just public—it's private. It's the quiet commitment to someone's well-being. It's the daily decision to stand with them. That's love in motion.

Advocacy also means consistency. It's not a one-time post or speech—it's a lifestyle. **Micah 6:8** says, "*What does the Lord require of you? To act justly and to love mercy and to walk humbly with your God.*" That's the rhythm of advocacy. It's justice, mercy, and humility working together. When you advocate, you reflect God's heart. You become a bridge, not a barrier. You become a voice, not an echo. You become a servant, not a savior. That's the power of love that speaks.

7. Avoid Assumption

Assumptions are shortcuts that often lead to misunderstanding. They bypass empathy and build walls instead of bridges. **Proverbs 18:2** says, "*Fools find no pleasure in understanding but delight in airing their own opinions.*" That's the danger of assumption—it replaces truth with presumption. When you assume, you stop listening. You stop learning. You stop loving. Jesus never assumed—He asked, He listened, He discerned. He saw each person as unique. He didn't treat the blind man like the leper. He didn't treat the Pharisee like the prostitute. He met each heart with fresh grace.

Avoiding assumptions requires intentionality. It means slowing down and seeking clarity. **James 1:5** says, "*If any of you lacks wisdom, you should ask God… and it will be given to you.*" Wisdom begins with humility. It begins with the willingness to say, "I don't know, but I want to understand." ***When you avoid assumptions, you honor someone's story. You give them space to speak. You*** *give them dignity*. You become a safe place. Assumptions are easy—but love is intentional. Love asks, listens, and learns.

To avoid assumption is to embrace curiosity. It's to say, "Tell me more." It's to lean in, not pull away. Jesus asked questions even when He knew the answers. He modeled humility. He modeled patience. He modeled love that seeks understanding. When you avoid assumptions, you build trust. You build a connection. You build peace. That's the fruit of empathy.

Avoiding assumptions also means checking your heart. **Matthew 7:1-2** says, *"Do not judge, or you too will be judged."* Judgment often begins with an assumption. But grace begins with listening. When you avoid assumptions, you choose love over labels. You choose truth over stereotypes. You choose connection over control. That's the posture of Christ. That's the power of humility. That's the beauty of grace.

8. Assist Where You Can

Assisting someone is love in action. It's saying, "I may not be able to do everything, but I'll do something." **Galatians 6:10** says, *"Therefore, as we have opportunity, let us do good to all people."* That's the call to help. Not when it's convenient—but when it's needed. Assistance doesn't have to be grand—it just has to be genuine. A kind word, a helping hand, a silent prayer—these are seeds of love. Jesus fed the hungry, healed the sick, and comforted the broken. He didn't wait for perfect conditions. He acted with compassion. That's our model.

Assisting means being available. It means saying, "Here I am, Lord—use me." **Isaiah 6:8** says, *"Here am I. Send me!"* That's the heart of a servant. You don't need a title to help—you need a heart. You don't need a platform—you need purpose. Assistance is not about being the hero—it's about being the helper. It's about showing up. It's about doing what you can with what you have. That's love in motion.

To assist is to reflect God's generosity. **2 Corinthians 9:11** says, *"You will be enriched in every way so that you can be generous on every occasion."* Generosity is not just financial—it's emotional, spiritual, and practical. When you assist, you become a channel of blessing. You become a vessel of grace. You become a light in someone's darkness. Assistance is not about fixing—it's about serving. It's about lifting burdens. It's about sharing hope.

Assisting also means being sensitive. It's asking, "What do you need?" not "What do I want to give?" It's listening before acting. It's discerning before deciding. Jesus didn't give everyone the same help—He tailored His love. That's wisdom. That's compassion. That's grace. When you assist where you can, you become a living sermon. You become a reflection of Christ. You become a blessing.

8

******

SPEAK LIFE, NOT LABELS

Words are powerful. They can build bridges or burn them, heal wounds or deepen them. In a world where criticism often comes quicker than compassion, many hearts are bruised by careless labels. We speak without thinking, forgetting that every word carries weight. **Proverbs 18:21** reminds us, *"Death and life are in the power of the tongue."* This chapter is a call to rise above the habit of hurting with our words and to become vessels of healing. It's not just about avoiding insults—it's about choosing to speak life, even when it's easier to judge. *When we label others, we limit them. But when we speak life, we unlock potential, restore dignity, and reflect the heart of Christ*. The journey begins with awareness, but it leads to transformation. Let us learn to speak with grace, seasoned with truth, and anchored in love.

Many people carry invisible wounds from words spoken over them—names they were called, judgments they couldn't shake, criticisms that became internal prisons. These labels often echo louder than the truth, shaping identity and stealing joy. But Jesus never labeled people by their failures. He saw the woman at the well not as broken, but as beloved. He called Zacchaeus not a thief, but a son. He spoke life into the dead places of people's hearts, and He invites us to do the same. Healing begins when we stop repeating the cycle of hurt and start releasing words that restore. **Ephesians 4:29** says, *"Let no corrupt communication proceed out of your mouth, but that which is good to the use of edifying."* Our words should lift, not crush. ***They should point to hope, not shame. And when we speak life, we become agents of change in a hurting world.***

This chapter will guide you through the process of replacing harmful habits with holy speech. You'll learn to recognize the roots of bad habits, respond with grace, and rebuild relationships through peaceful language. God is calling you to be a speaker of life, a messenger of mercy, and a builder of hearts. Let's begin the journey of healing the habit of hurting—one word at a time.

1. Compare

Comparison is not always about feeling less—it often comes from feeling more. A person who constantly compares may secretly believe they are better than others. They look down to feel lifted up. They measure others to maintain their own pride. This is not humility—it is hidden arrogance. **Luke 18:11** shows this clearly: *"God, I thank you that I am not like other people."* That Pharisee compared himself to feel righteous. But God rejected his pride. Comparison is a tool of the proud, not the humble. It creates division, not unity. It builds walls, not bridges. It is wise to rise above comparison and walk in love. You are above comparison when you walk in truth.

People who compare often criticize silently. They notice flaws in others to feel flawless themselves. They say, "I would never do that," or "I'm more spiritual than them." This is not wisdom—it is pride dressed as holiness. **Proverbs 16:18** warns, *"Pride goes before destruction."* Comparison blinds you to your own weaknesses. It makes you feel strong while others look weak. But strength in God is not found in comparison—it's found in compassion. When you compare, you stop growing. You become stuck in judgment. You lose the joy of your own journey. It is wise to focus on your path, not someone else's. You are above comparison when you walk in grace.

The person who compares often competes silently. They want to be first, best, and noticed. They see others as threats, not teammates. They feel superior and want to stay on top. But God does not bless prideful competition. **James 3:16** says, *"Where you have envy and selfish ambition, there you find disorder."* **Comparison creates chaos in the heart. It leads to jealousy, rivalry, and insecurity. The person who compares is not at peace.** They are chasing approval, not walking in purpose. True peace comes when you stop comparing and start celebrating. It is wise to lift others, not measure them. You are above comparison when you walk in purpose.

To break free from comparison, you must renew your mind. Stop looking around—start looking up. Stop measuring—start maturing. **Romans 12:3** says, *"Do not think of yourself more highly than you ought."* That means don't compare to feel superior. Instead, think with sober judgment. Know your worth, but don't use it to crush others. Celebrate your gifts, but honor theirs too. You are not better—you are blessed. You are not above people—you are above pride. Comparison is a distraction from destiny. It is wise to walk in humility and confidence. You are above comparison because you know who you are in Christ.

SYAVIHA MULENGYA

2. Compete

People who feel they are above others often live to win. They want to be first, best, and praised. They see life as a race, not a journey. They compare achievements and chase applause. But this mindset leads to stress and pride. **James 3:16** says, *"Where you have envy and selfish ambition, there you find disorder."* Competing for attention creates confusion. It breaks relationships. It builds walls between people. It makes you feel important but empty. It is wise to stop racing and start resting in God's plan. You are above competition when you walk in peace.

The person who competes often fears being forgotten. They want to be noticed and admired. They believe their worth comes from winning. But God does not reward prideful ambition. He honors faithfulness and love. **Philippians 2:3** says, *"Do nothing out of selfish ambition or vain conceit. Rather, in humility value others above yourselves."* That means true greatness comes from serving. Competing to feel superior leads to burnout. It also leads to broken trust. People who compete often struggle with jealousy. They cannot celebrate others. It is wise to choose purpose over pride. You are above competition when you serve with joy.

Competing makes you compare constantly. You look at others and feel threatened. You want to be better, faster, stronger. But this is not God's way. **1 Corinthians 9:24** reminds us, *"Run in such a way as to get the prize."* That prize is not fame—it's faithfulness. God wants you to run your own race. Not someone else's. When you compete, you lose focus. You chase titles instead of truth. You seek applause instead of approval from God. It is wise to run with grace, not greed. You are above competition when you trust your lane.

To break free from competition, renew your heart. Ask God to show you your true value. Stop chasing attention. Start building impact. Serve without needing credit. Love without needing applause. **Romans 12:10** says, *"Honor one another above yourselves."* That means lifting others is strength, not weakness. You don't need to win to matter. You just need to walk in obedience. God sees your heart, not your trophies. It is wise to live for His glory, not your own. You are above competition when you walk in love.

3. Condemn

People who feel superior often condemn others. They point out faults to feel righteous. They judge quickly and harshly. They believe they are better, cleaner, or more spiritual. But this is not the heart of God. **Luke 6:37** says, *"Do not judge, and you will not be judged. Do not condemn, and you will not be condemned."* Condemnation creates fear and shame. It pushes people away. It makes you feel powerful but proud. It is wise to choose mercy over judgment. You are above condemnation when you walk in grace.

The person who condemns often hides their own flaws. They focus on others to avoid looking inward. They speak with harshness, not healing. They use truth without love. But truth without love is dangerous. **John 8:7** reminds us, *"Let any one of you who is without sin be the first to throw a stone."* That means we all need grace. Condemning others does not make you holy. It makes you hard. **People who condemn often feel insecure.** They use judgment to protect their pride. It is wise to offer grace, not guilt. You are above condemnation when you forgive freely.

Condemnation breaks relationships. It creates fear, not faith. It makes people feel unworthy. But Jesus came to restore, not reject. **Romans 8:1** says, *"There is now no condemnation for those who are in Christ Jesus."* That means freedom is found in Him, not in judgment. People who condemn often feel they are above correction. But no one is perfect. We all need grace. It is wise to speak life, not labels. You are above condemnation when you walk in truth.

To break free from condemnation, choose compassion. See people through God's eyes. Speak with kindness. Correct with love. Forgive quickly. Pray for those who fall. **Galatians 6:1** says, *"Restore that person gently."* That means healing is better than hurting. You don't need to condemn to feel strong. You need to love to be wise. God honors mercy. He blesses the humble. You are above condemnation when you walk in mercy

4. Criticize

People who feel they are above others often criticize quickly. They see faults in everyone but themselves. They speak harshly and judge loudly. They believe their way is the best way. But this is not wisdom—it is pride. **Matthew 7:3** says, *"Why do you look at the speck of sawdust in your brother's eye and pay no attention to the plank in your own eye?"* That means we must examine ourselves first. Criticism without love is cruelty. It breaks hearts and builds walls. It makes you feel powerful but leaves others wounded. It is wise to speak with grace, not judgment. You are above criticism when you walk in love.

The person who criticizes often hides their own pain. They use harsh words to protect their pride. They feel strong when others look weak. But strength is not found in tearing others down. It is found in lifting them up. **Proverbs 15:1** says, *"A gentle answer turns away wrath, but a harsh word stirs up anger."* That means kindness is more powerful than criticism. People who feel superior often correct without compassion. They forget that everyone is growing.

They forget that God is patient with them too. It is wise to correct with care. You are above criticism when you walk in humility.

Criticism creates fear, not faith. It makes people afraid to speak or grow. It silences creativity and kills confidence. But God calls us to build, not break. **Ephesians 4:29** says, *"Do not let any unwholesome talk come out of your mouths, but only what is helpful for building others up."* That means our words should heal, not hurt. People who criticize often feel they are always right. But no one is perfect. We all need grace. We all need encouragement. It is wise to speak life. You are above criticism when you choose to bless.

To break free from criticism, change your words. Speak with kindness. Listen before you speak. Pray before you correct. Encourage often. Celebrate growth. **Proverbs 18:21** says, *"The tongue has the power of life and death."* That means your words matter. Use them to lift, not crush. Speak truth with love. Correct with gentleness. You are above criticism when you speak with wisdom.

5. Control

People who feel superior often try to control others. They want things done their way. They believe they know best. They struggle to trust others. But control leads to stress and conflict. **Proverbs 3:5** says, *"Trust in the Lord with all your heart and lean not on your own understanding."* That means we must let go and trust God. Control is rooted in fear. It says, "I must fix everything." But God is the one who holds all things together. It is wise to surrender control. You are above control when you walk in faith.

The person who controls often feels unsafe inside. They fear failure and rejection. They want to protect their image. They want

SYAVIHA MULENGYA

to avoid mistakes. But control does not bring peace. It brings pressure. **Isaiah 26:3** says, "You will keep in perfect peace those whose minds are steadfast, because they trust in You." That means peace comes from trust, not control. People who feel superior often believe they must lead everything. But leadership is not about control—it's about service. It is wise to release and rest. You are above control when you trust God's plan.

Control damage relationships. It makes others feel small. It creates tension and fear. It blocks creativity and freedom. But God calls us to love, not dominate. **Galatians 5:13** says, *"Serve one another humbly in love."* That means leadership must be gentle. People who control often resist change. They fear losing power. But true power is found in peace. It is wise to lead with love. You are above control when you walk in grace. To break free from control, surrender daily. Pray for peace. Trust God's timing. Let go of fear. Let others grow. Allow mistakes. **Romans 8:28** says, *"In all things God works for the good of those who love Him."* That means you don't have to fix everything. God is working. You can rest. You can release. You are above control when you walk in trust.

6. Complain

People who feel superior often complain often. They believe they deserve better. They focus on what's wrong. They speak with frustration. But complaining poisons the heart. **Philippians 2:14** says, *"Do everything without grumbling or arguing."* That means complaining is not God's way. It creates bitterness. It blocks blessings. It makes you feel stuck. It is wise to choose gratitude. You are above complaining when you walk in joy.

The person who complains often feels entitled. They expect perfection. They forget their blessings. They focus on problems. But gratitude opens the heart. **Psalm 100:4** says, "Enter His gates with thanksgiving and His courts with praise." *That means praise brings you closer to God.* Complaining pushes you away. People who feel superior often believe they deserve more. But humility says, "Thank You, Lord." It is wise to count your blessings. You are above complaining when you walk in praise.

Complaining spreads negativity. It affects your mood. It affects your relationships. It creates tension. It blocks peace. But God calls us to rejoice always. **1 Thessalonians 5:18** says, "Give thanks in all circumstances." That means even in hard times, we can be thankful. People who complain often miss what God is doing. They focus on lack, not love. They speak defeat, not destiny. It is wise to speak faith. You are above complaining when you trust God's goodness.

To break free from complaining, practice gratitude. Write down your blessings. Speak life daily. Praise God often. Thank Him for small things. Celebrate progress. Avoid negative talk. Surround yourself with joyful people. Read the Psalms. Sing songs of praise. You are above complaining when you choose joy.

9

****

BEING HARSH TO OTHER PEOPLE

Words are powerful. The Bible says, *"Death and life are in the power of the tongue"* (**Proverbs 18:21**). When we speak harshly, we may not see the wounds we cause, but they can cut deep into someone's heart. *Why Harsh Words Hurt* is not just about feelings—it's about the damage they can do to trust, love, and unity. *The Cost of Being Unkind* is high because our words can either build bridges or burn them. God calls us to *Speak to Heal, Not to Hurt*, to let our words be *"full of grace, seasoned with salt"* (**Colossians 4:6**), so they bring hope and healing.

The Lord warns us about *The Danger of a Sharp Tongue*. **James 1:19** reminds us to be *"quick to listen, slow to speak, and slow to become angry."* Choosing *Kindness Over Cruelty* is not weakness—it is strength under control. When we learn *Taming the Harsh Voice*, we open the door for *Gentle Words, Strong Impact* that can change lives. With God's help, we can start *Breaking the Cycle of Harshness* in our homes, churches, and communities. This is not just about speaking better—it's about loving better, because Jesus said, *"By this everyone will know that you are my disciples, if you love one another"* (**John 13:35**).

SYAVIHA MULENGYA

The Wounds We Cause Without Touching

1. Self-Righteousness

Self-righteousness makes people think they are better than others because they follow rules or live a clean life. In **John 8**, the religious leaders brought the woman to Jesus, hoping to trap Him and prove their own holiness. They were quick to point out her sin but blind to their own. Jesus did not praise their actions—He challenged their hearts. He said, *"Let him who is without sin among you be the first to throw a stone at her"* (**John 8:7**). That one sentence exposed their pride. They walked away, one by one, because they knew they were not perfect. Self-righteousness is dangerous because it hides behind religion. It uses God's law to condemn instead of to restore. But Jesus came to bring grace and truth. He showed that mercy is greater than judgment.

People who are self-righteous often speak loudly but love little. They quote Scripture to shame others but forget to apply it to themselves. The Pharisees used the law of Moses to accuse the woman, but they ignored God's heart. *"For all have sinned and fall short of the glory of God"* (**Romans 3:23**). That verse reminds us that no one is without fault. Jesus did not deny the woman's sin, but He did not let her be destroyed by it. He offered her a new beginning. Self-righteousness makes us proud and cold. It keeps us from seeing our need for grace. Jesus teaches us to look at our own hearts first. His way is full of love and truth.

When we act self-righteous, we forget that we need forgiveness too. We point fingers instead of opening our hands. We build walls instead of bridges. Jesus came to tear down those walls. "God opposes the proud but gives grace to the humble" (**James 4:6**). The Pharisees failed to see their own sin, but Jesus helped them see

SYAVIHA MULENGYA

the truth. He did not shame them—He invited them to change. Self-righteousness keeps us from growing. It makes us think we are already good enough. But God's Word shows us that we all need a Savior. Jesus is that Savior, full of mercy and grace.

Jesus did not condemn the woman. He said, *"Neither do I condemn you; go, and from now on sin no more"* (**John 8:11**). That is the heart of the gospel. We are not saved by being good—we are saved by grace. When we understand that, we become gentle with others. We stop judging and start loving. Jesus invites us to live with humility. He wants us to walk in truth and grace. Self-righteousness has no place in God's kingdom. Grace does.

2. Superiority

Superiority means thinking you are more important or better than someone else. The Pharisees acted like they were above the woman caught in adultery. They stood tall while she was thrown to the ground. They used her shame to lift themselves up. But Jesus did not join them. He bent down and wrote in the dust. His posture showed humility. *"Do nothing out of selfish ambition or vain conceit. Rather, in humility value others above yourselves"* (**Philippians 2:3**). Jesus did not act superior—He acted with compassion. He reminded them that everyone has sinned. His words made them think deeply.

When we feel superior, we stop listening to others. We think we know everything. The Pharisees did not ask Jesus for wisdom—they tried to trap Him. They thought they were better than the woman. But Jesus showed them they were not. *"There is no one righteous, not even one"* (**Romans 3:10**). Superiority makes us proud and cold. It keeps us from loving people well. Jesus teaches us to be humble. He wants us to serve, not to rule. God's Word calls us to walk in love and humility.

Superiority often comes from fear. We try to look strong so others won't see our weakness. The Pharisees feared losing their power. They used the woman's pain to protect their position. But Jesus was not impressed by titles or status. He looked at the heart. "Man looks at the outward appearance, but the Lord looks at the heart" (**1 Samuel 16:7**). He saw the woman's pain and the Pharisees' pride. He spoke truth to both. Superiority cannot live where grace is present. Grace brings everyone to the same level.

Jesus did not treat the woman as less. He spoke to her with kindness. He did not ignore her sin, but He did not define her by it. That is the power of love. It lifts the lowly and humbles the proud. We are called to walk in humility. To see others as equals. To serve with joy. "*Whoever wants to become great among you must be your servant*" (**Matthew 20:26**). Superiority has no place in the kingdom of God. Love does

3. Silencing Others

Silencing others is a way of taking away their voice and dignity. In the story, the woman was dragged into the crowd, but she was not allowed to speak. The religious leaders spoke for her, accused her, and used her pain to make a point. She was treated like an object, not a person. But Jesus did not let her stay silent. He gave her space to be seen and heard. *"Open your mouth for the mute, for the rights of all who are destitute"* (**Proverbs 31:8**). Jesus did not speak over her—He spoke to her. He looked at her with compassion. He gave her a voice when others tried to take it away. That is the heart of God.

SYAVIHA MULENGYA

When we silence others, we ignore their story. We assume we know everything and forget to listen. The Pharisees did not ask the woman what happened. They did not care about her pain or her past. But Jesus cared deeply. He listened with His heart. *"Everyone should be quick to listen, slow to speak and slow to become angry"* (**James 1:19**). Listening is an act of love. It shows respect and honor. Jesus teaches us to hear the broken, not just speak about them. He restores what others try to erase.

Silencing others can happen in many ways. It happens when we judge without understanding. It happens when we gossip, interrupt, or ignore someone's pain. The woman was silenced by shame, but Jesus broke that silence. He spoke life into her situation. *"The Lord is near to the brokenhearted and saves the crushed in spirit"* (**Psalm 34:18**). Jesus did not rush to speak—He paused to restore. His silence was powerful. It gave space for healing. He teaches us to be gentle with those who are hurting.

We are called to be people who listen and lift others. We must speak up for those who are silenced. We must create space for healing and hope. Jesus models this perfectly. He did not silence the woman—He empowered her. Her story became a testimony of grace. *"Speak up for those who cannot speak for themselves"* (**Proverbs 31:9**). We are called to be voices of compassion. To listen with love and speak with wisdom. Silencing others is not God's way. Restoration is.

4. Shaming

Shaming is when we make someone feel worthless because of their mistakes. The woman caught in adultery was publicly shamed. She was dragged into the crowd and exposed. Her sin was used to humiliate her. But Jesus did not join in the shaming. He protected her dignity. *"Love covers over a multitude of sins"* (**1 Peter 4:8**). Jesus did not ignore her sin, but He did not use it to destroy her. He showed grace instead of shame. He lifted her up when others wanted to tear her down. That is the love of God.

Shame makes people feel like they are beyond forgiveness. It tells them they are too broken to be healed. The Pharisees wanted the woman to feel hopeless. They wanted her to be punished and forgotten. But Jesus offered her a new beginning. *"There is now no condemnation for those who are in Christ Jesus"* (**Romans 8:1**). That verse is a promise of freedom. Jesus did not condemn her—He forgave her. He gave her a future. Shame says, "You are finished." Grace says, "You are forgiven."

Shaming others is not the way of Christ. It is the way of pride and fear. We shame people when we forget our own need for mercy. Jesus reminds us that we all fall short. *"Blessed is the one whose transgressions are forgiven, whose sins are covered"* (**Psalm 32:1**). The woman's sin was real, but so was God's mercy. Jesus did not throw stones—He offered peace. He teaches us to do the same. To cover others with love, not expose them with hate. Shaming is not healing. We must be people who restore, not shame. We must speak life, not death. Jesus shows us how to love the broken. He did not shame the woman—He saved her. Her story is a picture of grace. *"He heals the brokenhearted and binds up their wounds"* (**Psalm 147:3**). We are called to be healers. To lift the fallen and love the hurting. Shaming has no place in the heart of God. Mercy does.

5. Separating

Separating means pushing people away because of their mistakes or differences. The woman was separated from the crowd, not to be helped, but to be judged. She was treated as unworthy. The Pharisees wanted her to be cast out. But Jesus did not push her away—He drew near. *"Come to me, all who are weary and burdened, and I will give you rest"* (**Matthew 11:28**). Jesus invites the broken, not rejects them. He stood with her when others walked away. He brought her close when others wanted her gone. That is the heart of grace.

Separation creates loneliness and pain. It tells people they do not belong. The woman was isolated by shame, but Jesus brought her back into hope. He did not let her stay alone. *"God sets the lonely in families"* (**Psalm 68:6**). Jesus did not just forgive her—He restored her. He gave her a place again. He showed that no one is too far from His love. Separation is a tool of the enemy. Restoration is the work of God.

We often separate people because we fear their brokenness. We think their sin will stain us. But Jesus was not afraid of her sin. He stepped into her pain. *"For the Son of Man came to seek and to save the lost"* (**Luke 19:10**). He did not run from her—He rescued her. He teaches us to do the same. To welcome, not reject. To embrace, not exclude. Separation is not love.

We are called to be people of unity and grace. To bring others close, not push them away. Jesus shows us how to love without fear. He did not separate the woman—He saved her. Her story is a reminder that no one is too far gone. *"Accept one another, then, just as Christ accepted you"* (**Romans 15:7**). We must be bridges, not barriers. We must love with open arms. Separation is not God's way. Restoration is.

6. Superficiality

Superficiality means focusing on the outside and ignoring the heart. The Pharisees saw the woman's sin but not her soul. They judged her by her mistake, not her potential. Jesus looked deeper.

"People look at the outward appearance, but the Lord looks at the heart" (**1 Samuel 16:7**). He saw her pain, her story, and her need for grace. Superficial judgment is shallow and harmful. It misses the beauty of redemption. Jesus did not just see a sinner—He saw a daughter. He saw someone worth saving. That is the heart of God.

Superficiality leads to pride and blindness. It makes us think we are better than others. The Pharisees were dressed in religion but lacked compassion. Jesus saw through their masks. *"Woe to you… you clean the outside of the cup, but inside you are full of greed and self-indulgence"* (**Matthew 23:25**). He called out their hypocrisy. He did not praise their appearance—He challenged their hearts. True faith is not about looking holy—it's about being humble. Jesus teaches us to go deeper. To see people as God sees them.

We often fall into superficial thinking. We judge by clothes, status, or reputation. But Jesus teaches us to look beyond the surface. He saw the woman's brokenness and offered healing. *"The Lord is close to the brokenhearted"* (**Psalm 34:18**). He did not care about her image—He cared about her soul. That is the power of grace. It goes beneath the surface. It reaches the places others ignore. Jesus shows us how to love deeply. We must reject superficiality and embrace sincerity. We must see people with spiritual eyes. Jesus did not ignore the woman's sin, but He saw her worth. *"Above all else, guard your heart, for everything you do flows from it"* (**Proverbs 4:23**). The heart matters most. We are called to love from the inside out. To care more about character than appearance. Superficiality divides—sincerity heals. Jesus went deep, and so must we. That is the way of grace.

7. Stressing

Stressing means putting pressure on people instead of offering peace. The Pharisees stressed the law but ignored love. They demanded punishment and forgot mercy. Jesus did not add pressure—He brought peace. "Come to me, all who are weary and burdened, and I will give you rest" (**Matthew 11:28**). The woman was already broken—she did not need more weight. Jesus lifted her burden. He did not stress her—He saved her. That is the heart of the Gospel. Grace relieves, not crushes.

Stressing others comes from fear and control. We want people to change quickly, so we push them hard. But Jesus was patient and kind. He did not rush the woman—He restored her gently. "*The fruit of the Spirit is love, joy, peace, patience...*" (**Galatians 5:22**). He did not stress her with rules—He led her with love. His peace calmed the storm. His grace quieted the crowd. That is the way of Christ. He brings rest to the weary. We often stress people with expectations. We want perfection instead of progress. But Jesus celebrates every step forward. He did not demand the woman be perfect—He invited her to change. "*Go now and leave your life of sin*" (**John 8:11**). His words were freeing, not frightening. He gave her hope, not pressure. That is how transformation begins. With grace, not guilt. With peace, not panic.

We must be people of peace, not pressure. We must help others breathe, not break. Jesus shows us how to lead with love. "*Let the peace of Christ rule in your hearts*" (**Colossians 3:15**). The woman found peace in His presence. She was no longer stressed— she was saved. That is the power of grace. It lifts, not loads. We are called to be carriers of peace.

8. Speculation

Speculation means assuming things without knowing the truth. The Pharisees speculated about the woman's sin but never asked her story. They made conclusions without compassion. Jesus did not speculate—He saw clearly. *"Do not judge by appearances, but judge with right judgment"* (**John 7:24**). He did not guess—He knew. He did not assume—He understood. Speculation leads to misunderstanding and harm. It creates false stories and fuels gossip. Jesus teaches us to seek truth, not spread rumors. That is the way of love.

Speculation is dangerous. It turns people into headlines instead of humans. The woman was treated like a scandal, not a soul. But Jesus saw her heart. "Love rejoices with the truth" (**1 Corinthians 13:6**). He did not entertain gossip—He offered grace. He did not join the crowd—He stood apart. That is the power of discernment. Jesus teaches us to be wise, not reckless. To seek truth with love.

We often speculate when we lack facts. We fill in the blanks with fear or pride. But Jesus calls us to be careful with our words. *"The one who has knowledge uses words with restraint"* (**Proverbs 17:27**). He did not speak until He had something healing to say. He did not guess—He gave grace. That is the wisdom of God. It protects, not provokes. It listens before it speaks.

We must reject speculation and embrace truth. We must ask, not assume. Jesus shows us how to be careful and kind. *"Be quick to listen, slow to speak"* (**James 1:19**). The woman needed compassion, not conclusions. She needed grace, not gossip. Jesus gave her truth wrapped in love. That is our calling. To speak only what heals.

9. Stereotypes

Stereotypes are false labels that limit people. The woman was labeled by her sin, not her story. The crowd saw her as an adulteress, not a person. But Jesus saw her as a soul worth saving. *"So God created mankind in His own image"* (**Genesis 1:27**). She was more than her mistake. She was a child of God. Stereotypes blind us to beauty. They reduce people to roles. Jesus broke the label and restored her identity. That is the power of grace.

Stereotypes come from fear and ignorance. They make us judge without knowing. The Pharisees saw her as a sinner, but Jesus saw her as a daughter. *"There is neither Jew nor Gentile... for you are all one in Christ Jesus"* (**Galatians 3:28**). He did not divide—He united. He did not label—He loved. That is the heart of the Gospel. Jesus breaks barriers and builds bridges. He teaches us to see with love.

We often use stereotypes to feel safe. But they keep us from seeing people clearly. Jesus did not let labels define the woman. He gave her a new name—forgiven. *"You are a chosen people, a royal priesthood..."* (**1 Peter 2:9**). She was not just a sinner—she was a story of grace. That is what Jesus does. He rewrites our identity. He restores our worth.

We must reject stereotypes and embrace truth. We must see people as God sees them. Jesus did not let the crowd define the woman. He defined her with love. *"You are fearfully and wonderfully made"* (**Psalm 139:14**). That is the truth we must speak. No label can limit God's love. No stereotype can stop His grace. We are called to see with His eyes.

Become A Kind Person

1. Pause

Pausing is the first step to peace. When emotions rise, take a moment to breathe and reflect. A pause gives you time to think before you speak. It helps you avoid words that wound. Jesus modeled this when He paused to write on the ground before responding to the accusers (**John 8:6**). That silence shifted the atmosphere. Pausing invites the Holy Spirit to guide your response. It turns reaction into reflection. *"Be quick to listen, slow to speak, and slow to become angry"* (**James 1:19**). A pause is not weakness—it's wisdom.

When you pause, you create space for grace. You allow God to speak before you do. This moment of stillness can prevent regret. It can turn conflict into connection. Pausing helps you see the person, not just the problem. It reminds you that your words carry weight. Jesus didn't rush to condemn—He paused to restore. Let your silence be sacred. Let your pause be powerful. It's the beginning of gentleness.

2. Pray

Prayer is the pathway to a soft heart. When you feel harshness rising, take it to God. Prayer calms your spirit and clears your mind. It reminds you that you are not alone in your struggle. Jesus often withdrew to pray, even when surrounded by pressure (**Luke 5:16**). His prayers gave Him peace and strength. When you pray, you invite heaven into your heart. You ask God to help you respond with love. *"Create in me a clean heart, O God"* (**Psalm 51:10**). Prayer prepares you to speak with grace.

Prayer is not just asking—it's aligning. It aligns your heart with God's heart. It helps you see others through His eyes. When you pray for someone, it's harder to be harsh with them. Prayer softens your tone and strengthens your love. It turns frustration into forgiveness. *"Cast all your anxiety on Him because He cares for you"* (**1 Peter 5:7**). Let prayer be your first response, not your last resort. It's the secret to speaking with kindness. It's the solution to harshness.

SYAVIHA MULENGYA

3. Perceive

To perceive is to look beyond the surface. Harshness sees faults, but perception sees pain. Jesus saw the woman's heart, not just her mistake. He perceived her need for grace, not punishment. *"Man looks at the outward appearance, but the Lord looks at the heart"* (**1 Samuel 16:7**). When you perceive with love, you stop judging and start helping. You ask, "What's really going on inside?" That question opens the door to compassion. Perception leads to understanding. Understanding leads to healing.

We must train our eyes to see like Jesus. He saw brokenness and responded with mercy. He saw fear and offered peace. Perceiving means listening with your heart. It means noticing the silent cries behind loud actions. When you perceive, you become a peacemaker. You stop reacting and start restoring. *"The wisdom that comes from heaven is... considerate, submissive, full of mercy"* (**James 3:17**). Let your perception be guided by grace. See people as God sees them—worthy of love.

4. Personalize

Personalizing means putting yourself in someone else's shoes. It's asking, "How would I feel if I were them?" Harshness forgets that everyone has a story. Jesus personalized every encounter—He treated people with dignity. *"Do to others as you would have them do to you"* (**Luke 6:31**). When you personalize, you become more patient. You stop demanding and start understanding. You realize that people need grace, not judgment. Personalizing builds bridges, not walls. It turns criticism into compassion.

Jesus saw the woman not as a sinner to shame, but as a soul to save. He knew her pain and responded with peace. When you personalize, you reflect His love. You become a vessel of healing.

SYAVIHA MULENGYA

You stop pointing fingers and start lending hands. *"Carry each other's burdens, and in this way you will fulfill the law of Christ"* (**Galatians 6:2**). Personalizing helps you speak with kindness. It reminds you that everyone is fighting a battle you can't see. Let empathy lead your words. Let love guide your actions.

5. Pardon

Pardon means choosing to forgive, even when it's hard. Harshness holds grudges, but grace lets go. Jesus pardoned the woman caught in sin—He said, *"Neither do I condemn you"* (**John 8:11**). That pardon gave her a new beginning. Forgiveness is freedom—for you and for them. When you pardon, you release bitterness. You choose healing over hurting. *"Forgive as the Lord forgave you"* (**Colossians 3:13**). Pardon is not weakness—it's strength. It's the heart of the Gospel.

We all need pardon, and we all must give it. Jesus paid the price so we could be free. When you forgive, you reflect His love. You stop keeping score and start showing mercy. Pardon brings peace to your soul. It breaks the chains of anger and resentment. *"Blessed are the merciful, for they will be shown mercy"* (**Matthew 5:7**). Let forgiveness be your lifestyle. Speak words that heal, not hurt. Choose pardon, and you'll walk in peace.

6. Praise

Praise is the language of love. Harshness criticizes, but praise uplifts. Jesus praised faith, courage, and kindness wherever He saw it. He said, *"Your faith has healed you"* (**Mark 5:34**). Praise builds people up and helps them grow. It turns weakness into strength. It reminds others of their value. "Encourage one another and build each other up" (**1 Thessalonians 5:11**). Praise is powerful—it changes atmospheres. It brings joy where there was pain.

SYAVIHA MULENGYA

When you praise, you speak life. You help others see their potential. You become a voice of hope. Harshness tears down, but praise lifts up. Jesus used praise to affirm and inspire. He saw the good and celebrated it. *"The tongue has the power of life and death"* (**Proverbs 18:21**). Use your words to bless, not break. Let praise be your habit. It will transform your relationships.

7. Practice

Gentleness is not automatic—it's practiced. You won't get it perfect every time, but you can grow. Jesus practiced love daily, even with difficult people. He showed patience, kindness, and grace. *"Let your gentleness be evident to all"* (**Philippians 4:5**). Practice means trying again when you fail. It means choosing love even when it's hard. The more you practice, the more peace you carry. Harshness fades when gentleness grows. Practice makes progress.

Every day is a chance to practice grace. Speak kindly, listen deeply, and forgive quickly. Practice turns good intentions into holy habits. It builds character and deepens love. Jesus didn't just teach gentleness—He lived it. *"Follow God's example… and walk in the way of love"* (**Ephesians 5:1–2**). Let your life be a practice of peace. Don't wait for perfection—start with progress. The more you practice, the more you reflect Christ. Let gentleness be your daily goal.

10

******

RECOGNIZE THE BLESSING
IN YOUR LIFE

Every day, we walk through life surrounded by blessings—some we notice, many we overlook. From the way we look to the people we know, from the wisdom we carry to the wealth we steward, everything we have is a gift from God. These blessings are not earned by effort alone—they are expressions of divine grace. When we pause to reflect, we begin to see that our appearance, achievements, age, awards, authority, abilities, associations, assets, abundance, and assignments are not random—they are sacred deposits from heaven. They are not just signs of success—they are symbols of God's favor and fingerprints of His faithfulness.

God has given us beauty to reflect His creativity, success to fulfill His purpose, and years to testify of His goodness. He has placed us in positions of influence, surrounded us with people of impact, and equipped us with talents to serve. He has filled our hands with resources, our hearts with wisdom, and our lives with opportunities to make a difference. *"What do you have that you did not receive?"* (**1 Corinthians 4:7**). This question humbles us. It reminds us that every good thing comes from above. Our work, our wardrobe, our wallet, our winning strategies, and our wisdom are not products of pride—they are gifts of grace. When we recognize this truth, we stop boasting and start blessing. We stop comparing and start praising. Gratitude becomes our posture, and worship becomes our response.

Recognize, rejoice, and respond. Recognize the grace behind every gift. Rejoice in the goodness of God with a thankful heart. And respond with humility, praise, and purpose. Let your blessings lead you to worship, not pride. Let your success point to the Savior, not self. Let your influence be used to lift others, not elevate yourself. As you read through each section, may your heart be stirred to count your gifts, hear God's voice, and honor Him with all you have. Because when you truly see your blessings, you'll live with deeper gratitude, greater impact, and lasting joy. You are blessed—and you are called to be a blessing.

1. Appearance (Good Looking)

Your appearance is not just a result of genetics—it's a gift from God. Whether it's your smile, your posture, or your presence, it reflects the creativity of your Creator. *"I praise You because I am fearfully and wonderfully made"* (**Psalm 139:14**). When people admire your looks, remember to point upward. Beauty fades, but grace remains. God gave you your face, your features, and your glow. Use them to shine His love. Don't boast—bless. Don't compare—give thanks. Your appearance is a mirror of God's artistry.

Being good-looking is not a reason to feel proud—it's a reason to feel grateful. Many people struggle with self-image, but you can be a voice of encouragement. When you recognize your beauty as a gift, you stop seeking validation from others. You start honoring God with confidence and humility. *"Charm is deceptive, and beauty is fleeting; but a woman who fears the Lord is to be praised"* (**Proverbs 31:30**). Let your beauty reflect your heart. Let your face shine with kindness. Let your presence bring peace. You are beautiful because God made you.

Use your appearance to serve, not to show off. Smile at the hurting. Stand tall for the weak. Dress with dignity and grace. Your wardrobe is a gift—your style can speak life. *"Do not let your adornment be merely outward... but the hidden person of the heart"* (**1 Peter 3:3–4**). Let your beauty be a blessing. Let your look be a light. You are not just good-looking—you are God-crafted. Honor Him with your image.

2. Achievement

Every achievement is a testimony of God's grace. Whether you finished a book, earned a degree, or reached a goal, it was God who gave you strength. *"It is God who arms me with strength and makes my way perfect"* (**Psalm 18:32**). You didn't get there alone—He walked with you. Celebrate, but stay humble. Achievements are not medals—they are messages of mercy. They remind you that God is faithful. He opens doors, gives wisdom, and sends helpers. Your success is a seed—plant it with praise.

Achievements can tempt us to boast, but humility keeps us grounded. When people applaud you, bow your heart before God. Say, "Lord, thank You for helping me." *"Let the one who boasts boast in the Lord"* (**Jeremiah 9:24**). Your trophies are temporary, but your testimony is eternal. Use your achievements to inspire others. Share your story, but highlight God's hand. You climbed the mountain, but He gave you the legs. You wrote the book, but He gave you the words. Stay humble, stay grateful.

SYAVIHA MULENGYA

Let your achievements serve a purpose beyond yourself. Use them to build, bless, and bring hope. Teach others what you've learned. Encourage those who are still climbing. *"Whatever you do, do it all for the glory of God"* (**1 Corinthians 10:31**). Your success is a platform—stand on it with praise. Your accomplishments are arrows—point them to heaven. You are not just successful—you are sent. Honor God with every win.

3. Age

Your age is a gift, whether you are young or old. Every year you live is a testimony of God's protection. *"Even to your old age and gray hairs I am He who will sustain you"* (**Isaiah 46:4**). Don't complain about getting older—celebrate it. Many didn't make it this far. Your age means you've seen God's faithfulness. You've survived storms and grown stronger. You've gained wisdom and walked through grace. Your age is not a burden—it's a blessing. Count your years with gratitude.

Youth is a gift, but so is maturity. When you're young, honor God with energy and dreams. *"Don't let anyone look down on you because you are young…"* (**1 Timothy 4:12**). When you're older, honor God with wisdom and legacy. Age brings perspective, patience, and purpose. Don't envy others—embrace your season. God uses every stage for His glory. Whether you're 20 or 70, you have a role to play. Your age is your assignment.

Use your age to teach, testify, and trust. Share your journey with others. Speak life into the next generation. Show them how God carried you. *"Teach us to number our days, that we may gain a heart of wisdom"* (**Psalm 90:12**). Your age is not just a number—it's a narrative. It tells the story of grace. Honor God with your years. Live each day with purpose.

SYAVIHA MULENGYA

4. Award

Awards are symbols of recognition, but the real reward is God's favor. When you receive an award, remember who gave you the ability. *"Every good and perfect gift is from above"* (**James 1:17**). You didn't earn it alone—God equipped you. Awards are not just for display—they're for testimony. They show that excellence is possible through grace. They remind you to stay humble. Don't let awards inflate your ego—let them increase your gratitude. Your award is a reminder of God's hand. Celebrate, but stay surrendered.

Awards can open doors, but only God opens hearts. Use your recognition to reflect His goodness. Say, "This is not just my achievement—it's God's grace." *"Let another praise you, and not your own mouth"* (**Proverbs 27:2**). Your award is a tool—use it to build others. Don't chase trophies—chase truth. Don't seek applause—seek purpose. Your reward in heaven is greater than any plaque on earth. Stay focused on eternal impact.

Let your awards become altars of praise. Every time you see them, thank God. Share the story behind the success. Inspire others to trust God in their journey. *"Whatever you do, work at it with all your heart, as working for the Lord..."* (**Colossians 3:23**). Your award is not the end—it's a beginning. Use it to serve, speak, and shine. You are not just awarded—you are anointed. Honor God with your recognition.

5. Authority

Authority is a sacred trust from God. Whether you lead a team, a ministry, or a family, your position is a gift. *"There is no authority except that which God has established"* (**Romans 13:1**). You are not in charge by accident—God placed you there. Use your authority to serve, not to control. Lead with love, not pride. Speak with wisdom, not arrogance. Your authority is a platform for grace. Be a leader who listens to God.

Authority should never make you harsh—it should make you humble. Jesus had all authority, yet He washed feet (**John 13:5**). That's the model of true leadership. When you recognize your authority as a gift, you lead with compassion. You stop demanding and start discipling. You stop ruling and start reaching. *"Whoever wants to become great among you must be your servant"* (**Matthew 20:26**). Let your leadership reflect Christ. Let your influence bring healing.

Use your authority to lift others up. Empower, encourage, and equip. Speak life into those you lead. Make decisions with prayer and purpose. *"She opens her mouth with wisdom, and the teaching of kindness is on her tongue"* (**Proverbs 31:26**). Your authority is not about control—it's about calling. You are chosen to lead with love. Honor God with your position.

6. Ability

Your ability is a gift from God. Whether you sing, write, teach, or lead, it's not just talent—it's grace. *"We have different gifts, according to the grace given to each of us"* (**Romans 12:6**). You didn't choose your skills—God placed them in you. He gave you the strength to grow and the wisdom to use them. Your ability is not for pride—it's for purpose. Use it to serve, not to show off. Use it to bless, not to boast. Every time you use your gift, thank God. You are able because He is able. Your ability is a tool for impact.

Don't compare your ability to others—celebrate what God gave you. You may not do everything, but you can do something well. That "something" is your assignment. *"Each of you should use whatever gift you have received to serve others…"* (**1 Peter 4:10**).

Your ability is your ministry. It's how you shine light in dark places. It's how you bring hope to hurting hearts. God gave you your gift for a reason. Use it with humility and joy. Let your ability reflect His glory. You are gifted by grace.

Honor God with your ability every day. Practice it, protect it, and pour it out. Don't bury your talent—build with it. *"To whom much is given, much will be required"* (**Luke 12:48**). Your ability is a responsibility. Use it wisely and faithfully. Let your work speak of God's goodness. Let your skill point to the Savior. You are not just talented—you are trusted. Recognize the grace behind your gift. Praise God for your ability.

7. Association

The people you are connected to are part of God's plan. Your friends, mentors, and ministry partners are not accidents—they are assignments. "Bad company corrupts good character" (**1 Corinthians 15:33**), but good company builds strong faith. God places people in your life to sharpen, support, and stretch you. Your associations shape your future. Choose them wisely and thank God for them. Don't take relationships for granted—they are gifts. Every connection is a chance to grow. Every friendship is a seed of grace. Your circle matters.

Be humble in your associations. Don't think you're better than others—see everyone as valuable. Jesus associated with the poor, the broken, and the rejected. He showed love to all, not just the powerful. *"Do not be proud, but be willing to associate with people of low position"* (**Romans 12:16**). Your attitude in relationships reveals your heart. Honor those around you. Listen, learn, and love well. Your associations are opportunities to reflect Christ. Be a blessing in every bond.

SYAVIHA MULENGYA

Use your associations to build the Kingdom. Collaborate, encourage, and pray together. Don't isolate—connect with purpose. *"Two are better than one… if either of them falls, one can help the other up"* (**Ecclesiastes 4:9–10**). Your relationships are part of your calling. They help you grow and go further. Recognize the grace in every connection. Thank God for the people He's placed in your life. You are surrounded by grace. Honor God through your associations.

8. Asset

Your assets—money, property, tools—are gifts from God. You may have a house, a car, or a phone, but they are not just possessions—they are provisions. *"The earth is the Lord's, and everything in it"* (**Psalm 24:1**). Everything you own belongs to God first. He gave it to you to manage, not to worship. Be a faithful steward, not a selfish owner. Use your assets to serve others. Share, give, and bless. Your assets are not just for comfort—they are for calling. Recognize the grace in what you have.

Don't let your assets make you proud—let them make you generous. God blesses you so you can bless others. *"Honor the Lord with your wealth…"* (**Proverbs 3:9**). Your wallet is a tool for worship. Your home is a place for hospitality. Your resources are meant to reflect God's heart. Be wise with what you have. Don't waste—invest in eternity. Let your assets serve your assignment. You are rich in grace.

Praise God for every asset, big or small. Whether it's a laptop or a microphone, use it for His glory. Let your possessions have purpose. *"You will be made rich in every way so that you can be generous…"* (**2 Corinthians 9:11**). Your assets are not just blessings—they are bridges. They connect you to people and purpose. Recognize the grace behind every gift. Be humble, be thankful, be generous. Your assets are from God—honor Him with them.

9. Abundance

Abundance is more than having a lot—it's having enough and more to share. God is the source of overflow. *"My cup overflows"* (**Psalm 23:5**). When you have abundance, it's not just for you—it's for others. Share your blessings with joy. Don't hoard—help. Don't boast—bless. God gives abundance to those who will use it wisely. Recognize that every extra is a gift. Be thankful for the overflow. Let your abundance be a testimony.

Abundance should lead to humility, not pride. You didn't earn it alone—God provided it. *"You may say, 'My power and the strength of my hands have produced this wealth,' but remember the Lord your God..."* (**Deuteronomy 8:17–18**). Stay grounded in grace. Use your abundance to lift others. Feed the hungry, clothe the poor, support the mission. Your abundance is a tool for transformation. It's not about luxury—it's about legacy. Be a channel, not a container. Let God's grace flow through you.

Honor God with your abundance every day. Give freely, live simply, and love deeply. *"Give, and it will be given to you... a good measure, pressed down, shaken together and running over..."* (**Luke 6:38**). Your abundance is a sign of God's favor. Use it to build His Kingdom. Don't waste the overflow—work it for good. Recognize the grace in every blessing. Be humble in plenty. Praise God for your abundance.

10. Assignment

Your assignment is your divine purpose. It's the work God gave you to do. Whether you preach, write, sing, or serve, it's not just a job—it's a calling. *"We are God's workmanship, created in Christ Jesus to do good works…"* (**Ephesians 2:10**). Your assignment is sacred. It's designed by God and powered by grace. Don't take it lightly—take it seriously. You are chosen for a reason. Your assignment is your mission. Recognize the grace in your calling.

Be humble in your assignment. You are not better than others—you are simply called. Jesus fulfilled His assignment with love and sacrifice. He said, *"I have brought You glory on earth by finishing the work You gave Me to do"* (**John 17:4**). Follow His example. Serve with joy, not pride. Work with excellence, not ego. Your assignment is not about fame—it's about faithfulness. Stay focused and faithful. Your calling is a gift.

Honor God through your assignment every day. Wake up with purpose and passion. Let your work reflect His wisdom. *"Whatever you do, work at it with all your heart, as working for the Lord…"* (**Colossians 3:23**). Your assignment is your altar. Offer it to God with praise. Let your life speak of His grace. You are not just working—you are worshiping. Recognize the grace in your assignment. Praise God for your purpose.

11

****

ACTORS IN THE CHURCH

Acting Holy, Living Empty

Some people in the church are like actors on a stage—they know how to look holy on the outside, but their hearts are far from God. Jesus said, *"These people honor me with their lips, but their hearts are far from me"* (**Matthew 15:8**). When we wear masks in God's house, pretending to be something we are not, we risk hypocrisy in the church. God is not impressed by a performance; He desires truth in the inward parts (**Psalm 51:6**). He is looking for believers who worship Him in spirit and in truth (**John 4:24**), not pretenders in the pews.

It is time to move from stage to sincerity. We must take off the mask, repent of false living, and let our faith be real both in public and in private. The world is watching, and Jesus said, "By this everyone will know that you are my disciples, if you love one another" (**John 13:35**). Let us live with real faith, not role-play, so that our lives match the message we preach. When our hearts are right with God, our actions will shine His light, and our witness will draw others to Christ.

SYAVIHA MULENGYA

Church is meant to be a place of love, truth, and healing. But sometimes, people come not to worship, but to perform. T*hey say the right things, smile at the right time, and act holy—but their hearts are far from God.* These are the actors in the Church. They wear masks of kindness, but behind the mask is pride, jealousy, or selfishness. This chapter is not to judge anyone, but to help us all look inside. Are we real in our faith, or are we just playing a role? God sees beyond our words and actions—He looks at the heart. He wants honesty, not performance. He wants love that is true, not fake. Let us take off the mask. Let us stop pretending. Let us be real with God, with others, and with ourselves. Because the Church doesn't need actors—it needs believers who live what they preach.

Hypocrisy is a silent destroyer. It wears the robe of righteousness but walks in deception. Many people speak of love, kindness, and faith, yet their actions betray a different reality. Jesus warned us about this danger, saying, *"Beware of the yeast of the Pharisees, which is hypocrisy"* (**Luke 12:1**). Hypocrisy is not just a flaw—it's a spiritual sickness. It poisons relationships, weakens churches, and misrepresents the heart of God. It is possible to look holy and live hollow. God is not impressed by appearances; He searches the heart. When care is fake, it causes confusion and pain. This message is not to condemn, but to awaken. We must learn to spot the signs and walk in truth.

When Worship Becomes a Show

True love is active, honest, and humble. Hypocrisy, on the other hand, is passive, proud, and pretentious. It speaks loudly but loves quietly. It offers help with hidden motives. It comforts with words but avoids sacrifice. The Bible says, *"Let love be without hypocrisy. Abhor what is evil; cling to what is good"* (**Romans 12:9**). God desires sincere hearts, not staged performances. Hypocrites often

SYAVIHA MULENGYA

care when it's convenient, not when it's costly. They help to be seen, not to serve. They speak of compassion but avoid commitment. This teaching will expose those patterns and call us to a higher standard.

We live in a time when image is valued more than integrity. Social media has made it easy to pretend, to polish, and to perform. But God is not fooled by filters or phrases. He sees the truth behind every post, every prayer, and every promise. Hypocrisy is not just in the world—it can creep into the church, the family, and even our own hearts. That's why Jesus spoke so strongly against it. He didn't just challenge behavior—He confronted motives. This message is a mirror, not a weapon. It helps us examine ourselves and grow in grace.

In this book, we will explore ten powerful signs of hypocrisy— each beginning with the letter "P." These signs will help you identify fake concern, shallow love, and selfish motives. But more importantly, they will guide you toward authentic care, godly compassion, and true humility. Each chapter will be rooted in Scripture, filled with insight, and written in simple language. Whether you are a leader, a believer, or someone seeking truth, this message will challenge and change you. Let us not be actors in the faith—let us be ambassadors of love. The world needs real hope, not rehearsed kindness. And God is calling us to live with clean hands and pure hearts.

1. Performance – Acting Like You Care

Some people don't care, but they act like they do. They speak kindly, but their heart are cold. They help only when others are watching. Their actions are for applause, not for love. Jesus warned us about this kind of behavior. He said, *"Be careful not to do your good deeds publicly to be admired by others"* (**Matthew 6:1**). True care is quiet and sincere. It doesn't need a stage or spotlight. Hypocrites want attention, not transformation. God sees through the performance and judges the heart.

A person who performs care is not truly loving. They say the right words but never follow through. They offer help but avoid sacrifice. Their kindness is shallow and short-lived. They care when it's easy, not when it's costly. Jesus called out the Pharisees for this exact behavior. He said, *"Everything they do is for show"* (**Matthew 23:5**). They looked holy but lacked mercy. They wanted honor, not humility. Real love doesn't need an audience—it needs a heart.

You can spot a performer by their patterns. They show up when it benefits them. They disappear when no one is watching. They speak with passion but act with pride. Their concern is selective and self-serving. They avoid messy situations and hard truths. They care when it's convenient, not consistent. Their love is loud but empty. God calls us to love in truth, not in drama. Let your care be real, even when no one sees it.

2. Pretense – Faking Concern

Some people pretend to care, but their hearts are far away. They say, "I'm here for you," but they never show up. Their words are smooth, but their actions are missing. Pretense is a mask that hides the truth. Jesus said, *"These people honor me with their lips, but their hearts are far from me"* (**Matthew 15:8**). Hypocrites know how to sound loving. They use spiritual language to cover selfish motives. They want to appear kind, not be kind. God is not fooled by fake concern. He looks at the heart, not the speech.

Pretenders often show up in public but vanish in private. They care when others are watching. They avoid deep conversations and real burdens. Their love is surface-level and short-lived. They don't weep with those who weep. They don't rejoice with those who rejoice. Their care is cold, calculated, and distant. True love enters pain and stays present. God calls us to love with truth, not with a mask. Pretense is a lie dressed in kindness.

You can spot pretense by its lack of depth. It avoids sacrifice and commitment. It disappears when things get hard. It speaks but never listens. It comforts with clichés, not compassion. It offers help but never follows through. It uses people instead of serving them. Jesus never pretended—He loved fully and freely. He touched the untouchable and embraced the broken. Let us reject pretense and choose real love.

3. Pride – Caring to Be Seen

Pride turns care into a performance. It helps others to feel important. It gives to be praised, not to bless. Jesus warned against this attitude. He said, *"Do not do your acts of righteousness before men to be seen by them"* (**Matthew 6:1**). Pride wants recognition, not relationship. It seeks applause, not healing. It uses kindness as a tool for self-promotion. God resists the proud but gives grace to the humble. True care is humble and hidden.

Prideful people care when it boosts their image. They post sympathy online but ignore real needs offline. They speak loudly but love quietly. They want to be known as kind, not actually be kind. They help only when it benefits them. They avoid messy situations that don't bring glory. They care when it's convenient and visible. Jesus humbled Himself to serve others. He washed feet, healed the sick, and welcomed sinners. Real love doesn't need a spotlight.

You can recognize pride by its hunger for attention. It brags about helping others. It keeps a score of good deeds. It expects praise for every act of kindness. It avoids serving in silence. It chooses status over sacrifice. Jesus said, *"Whoever wants to be great must be a servant"* (**Matthew 20:26**). Pride cannot love deeply—it only loves itself. God calls us to serve without seeking credit. Let your care be quiet, faithful, and free from pride.

4. Passive – Saying You Care but Doing Nothing

Passive care is empty care. It listens but never acts. It nods but never moves. It says, "I'll pray for you," but forgets. James said, *"Faith without works is dead"* (**James 2:17**). True love takes action. Hypocrites talk but don't help. They avoid involvement and responsibility. They feel sympathy but not urgency. God wants love that works, not just words.

Passive people avoid hard situations. They don't want to get involved. They fear discomfort more than they value compassion. They wait for others to act first. They delay help until it's too late. They offer advice but not assistance. They speak peace but don't bring it. Jesus didn't wait—He moved with compassion. He fed the hungry, healed the sick, and comforted the broken. Love must move, or it's not love at all.

You can spot passivity by its silence in crisis. It watches but doesn't weep. It hears but doesn't respond. It avoids the burden of care. It chooses comfort over commitment. It hides behind good intentions. Jesus said, "Whatever you did not do for one of the least of these, you did not do for me" (**Matthew 25:45**). Passive care is dangerous—it leaves people hurting. God calls us to be active in love. Let your care be bold, not passive.

5. Profit – Helping for Personal Gain

Some people help only when there's something to gain. They care when it benefits their reputation or wallet. Their kindness is a transaction, not a gift. They give to be praised, not to bless. Jesus saw this in the Pharisees and rebuked them. He said, *"They devour widows' houses and for a show make lengthy prayers"* (**Luke 20:47**). Hypocrites use compassion as a business strategy. They want influence, not intimacy. They help to climb higher, not to lift others. God sees the motive behind every act.

Profit-driven care is not love—it's manipulation. It looks generous but feels empty. It serves with strings attached. It expects rewards and recognition. True love gives freely and joyfully. Jesus said, *"Freely you have received; freely give"* (**Matthew 10:8**). Hypocrites count the cost before they care. They ask, "What's in it for me?" They use people as stepping stones. God calls us to serve without seeking gain.

You can spot profit-driven care by its conditions. It disappears when the benefits stop. It avoids the poor and broken. It favors the powerful and wealthy. It chooses status over sacrifice. It praises those who can repay. **Jesus served the least, the lost, and the lonely.** He gave without expecting anything back. Let your care be pure, not profitable. Love should never be for sale.

6. Polish – Looking Good but Lacking Heart

Some people look holy but live hollow. They polish their image but neglect their soul. They dress well, speak well, and act well—on the surface. Jesus said, *"You are like whitewashed tombs... beautiful on the outside but full of dead bones"* (**Matthew 23:27**). Hypocrites care more about appearance than authenticity. They want to be admired, not transformed. They clean the outside but ignore the inside. Their kindness is cosmetic, not spiritual. God desires truth in the inward parts. He looks beyond the polish.

Polished care is shallow and scripted. It follows trends, not truth. It copies others but lacks conviction. It avoids vulnerability and real emotion. It's more about branding than blessing. Jesus never cared about looking perfect. He touched lepers, cried with mourners, and walked with sinners. He showed messy, honest love. Hypocrites fear being real. God honors those who love from the heart.

You can recognize polish by its obsession with image. It avoids brokenness and weakness. It hides flaws instead of healing them. It speaks in rehearsed phrases. It fears judgment more than God. It values reputation over righteousness. Jesus said, *"Blessed are the pure in heart"* (**Matthew 5:8**). Polish fades, but purity lasts. Let your care be honest, not edited. God wants hearts, not performances.

7. Partiality – Caring for Some, Ignoring Others

Partiality is selective love. It chooses who to care for based on status or benefit. It favors the rich and ignores the poor. James warned against this in the church. He said, *"If you show favoritism, you sin"* (**James 2:9**). Hypocrites love those who look like them. They avoid the outcast and the broken. They care when it's comfortable. They reject those who challenge them. God's love is for all people.

Partial care creates division and pain. It builds walls instead of bridges. It judges by appearance, not by heart. It praises the popular and forgets the lonely. Jesus broke every barrier. He welcomed Samaritans, tax collectors, and sinners. He showed that love has no favorites. Hypocrites limit their compassion. They care for convenience, not conviction. God calls us to love without limits.

You can spot partiality by its patterns. It avoids the needy and embraces the powerful. It serves those who can repay. It ignores those who are different. It chooses comfort over calling. Jesus said, *"Whatever you did for the least of these, you did for me"* (**Matthew 25:40**). Partiality is not love—it's pride. Let your care be wide and welcoming. God's love reaches everyone. So should yours.

8. Pretending – Imitating Love Without Feeling It

Pretending is showing care without truly meaning it. It copies the actions of love but lacks the heart behind them. Words may sound kind, but they carry no weight. Jesus said, *"Out of the abundance of the heart the mouth speaks"* (**Luke 6:45**), reminding us that real love flows from within. Hypocrisy speaks of compassion but refuses to live it. It offers comfort without commitment and sympathy without sincerity. Pretending is often used to blend in, not to build up. But God sees past the surface—He desires truth, not performance. When we fake love, we dishonor the very nature of God, who is love. Pretending may fool people for a moment, but it cannot fool the One who sees the heart. Genuine love is not a show—it's a sacrifice.

Pretending is dangerous because it misleads and wounds. It gives the impression of care, then disappears when it's needed most. It builds false hope and leaves behind broken trust. Kindness becomes a mask, not a mission. It avoids real connection and keeps relationships shallow. Jesus never pretended—He loved with depth, honesty, and action. He wept with the hurting, healed the broken, and embraced the rejected. Hypocrisy fears emotional risk and chooses distance over devotion. But God calls us to love with courage and sincerity. *"Let your 'Yes' be 'Yes,' and your 'No,' 'No'"* (**Matthew 5:37**). Real love shows up, stays present, and speaks truth with grace.

SYAVIHA MULENGYA

9. Projection – Accusing Others to Hide Your Own Faults

Projection is blaming others to hide your own flaws. It points fingers to avoid accountability. It accuses others of being uncaring while being cold inside. Jesus said, *"Why do you look at the speck in your brother's eye and ignore the plank in your own?"* (**Matthew 7:3**). Hypocrites deflect attention from their own hearts. They criticize others to feel righteous. They use judgment to cover guilt. They pretend to care by condemning others. God sees the truth behind the words. He calls us to examine ourselves first.

Projection creates division and distrust. It breaks relationships and builds pride. It avoids repentance and embraces blame. It speaks loudly but listens poorly. Jesus taught humility, not hypocrisy. He said, *"Judge not, or you too will be judged"* (**Matthew 7:1**). Hypocrites use others as mirrors. They reflect their own faults onto others. True love corrects gently and humbly. God honors those who confess, not those who accuse.

You can spot projection by its harshness. It lacks grace and understanding. It criticizes without compassion. It avoids self-reflection. It speaks more about others than itself. Jesus said, *"First take the plank out of your own eye"* (**Matthew 7:5**). Projection is pride in disguise. Let your care begin with humility. God wants truth, not blame. Love starts with looking inward.

10. Paralysis – Feeling Compassion but Never Acting

Paralysis is when you feel something but do nothing. It's frozen love—real emotion with no movement. It says, "I care," but never proves it. James said, *"If you see someone in need and do nothing, what good is that?"* (**James 2:16**). Hypocrites feel but don't follow through. They are touched but not transformed. They are stirred but stay still. They delay action until it's too late. God wants love that moves. Compassion must lead to commitment.

Paralyzed care is dangerous. It comforts but never changes anything. It watches suffering and stays silent. It feels deeply but acts slowly. Jesus moved with compassion. He healed, fed, and embraced. He didn't wait—He walked toward pain. Hypocrites wait for perfect conditions. They care in theory, not in practice. God calls us to act in love.

You can spot paralysis by its hesitation. It talks but doesn't touch. It plans but never pursues. It feels but never finishes. It avoids risk and responsibility. Jesus said, *"Go and do likewise"* (**Luke 10:37**). Paralysis is love without legs. Let your care be active and alive.

12

****

BLESSED TO BE A BLESSING

We all receive blessings in life—some big, some small. But those blessings are not just for us to enjoy; they are meant to be shared. God gives us love, grace, and gifts so we can pass them on to others. When we help, encourage, and care for people around us, we show the heart of God. Being a blessing doesn't require wealth or fame—it simply takes a willing heart. A kind word, a helping hand, or a listening ear can make a big difference. The Bible reminds us in **Genesis 12:2**, *"I will bless you… and you will be a blessing."* That promise still speaks to us today. We are called to live with open hands and open hearts. When we bless others, we reflect God's goodness. And in doing so, we discover the joy of living with purpose.

1. Share

Sharing is one of the most beautiful ways to bless others. It is not just about giving money or material things—it is about sharing love, wisdom, and time. **Hebrews 13:16** says, *"Do not forget to do good and to share with others, for with such sacrifices God is pleased."* Sharing reminds people that they are loved and not forgotten.

SYAVIHA MULENGYA

When we hold onto everything for ourselves, we miss the opportunity to make a difference in someone's life. Many people struggle in silence, not because they lack ability, but because they lack support. **Proverbs 22:9** reminds us, *"The generous will themselves be blessed, for they share their food with the poor."* True joy comes from giving freely, expecting nothing in return.

Sharing is not just about what we give—it is about the impact we make. When we share love, we create warmth. When we share encouragement, we build confidence. When we share time, we strengthen relationships. What we share today can bless someone for a lifetime.

2. Support

Support means standing with people when they need it the most. Life is full of struggles, and sometimes, all a person needs is someone to remind them that they are not alone. Support does not always mean solving problems—it can be as simple as listening, encouraging, or offering a kind word. **Galatians 6:2** tells us, *"Carry each other's burdens, and in this way, you will fulfill the law of Christ."* This verse teaches us that support is an act of love, a way to share the weight of life's challenges so no one feels abandoned.

Many people go through difficulties in silence. They do not ask for help because they believe no one will care. But even the smallest act of kindness can make a difference. ***A smile, a phone call, or a word of encouragement can bring comfort to someone who is struggling***. **Romans 15:1** reminds us, *"We who are strong ought to bear with the failings of the weak and not to please ourselves."* This means that those who have strength should use it to lift others up, rather than looking down on them.

True support is not about grand gestures—it is about being present, about showing people they are seen and valued. Sometimes, people do not need advice or solutions; they simply need reassurance that they are not alone. **1 Thessalonians 5:11** says, *"Encourage one another and build each other up."* A world filled with encouragement is a world where people feel safe, loved, and empowered.

Supporting others also strengthens relationships. When people help one another, they build trust and deepen their connections. Friendships grow, families become stronger, and communities thrive. **Proverbs 17:17** tells us, *"A friend loves at all times, and a brother is born for a time of adversity."* Support is a gift that keeps relationships strong.

Ultimately, supporting others blesses us, too. When we choose to be kind and caring, we create an atmosphere of love and unity. Helping someone else does not weaken us—it makes us stronger, more compassionate, and more connected. **Luke 6:38** reminds us, *"Give, and it will be given to you."* A world where people support one another is a world filled with hope and peace.

3. Solve

Solving problems is another way to bless others. Life is full of challenges, and sometimes, people do not know how to move forward. Offering wisdom, guidance, or a helping hand can be life-changing. **Proverbs 3:27** says, *"Do not withhold good from those to whom it is due, when it is in your power to act."* This verse reminds us that if we have the ability to help someone, we should do it.

Many people struggle alone because they think no one cares or that asking for help makes them weak. But having someone to help solve a problem can bring relief, clarity, and hope. **James 1:5** tells us, *"If any of you lacks wisdom, you should ask God, who gives generously to all without finding fault."* Wisdom is meant to be shared—it is a gift that grows when passed on to others.

Solving problems does not mean taking control of someone's life. It means guiding them, encouraging them to find solutions, and helping them see possibilities they may not have noticed before. Whether it is sharing advice, offering practical help, or simply listening, we can be a blessing by helping others navigate their struggles.

Helping solve problems also strengthens communities. When people come together to support one another, they build a culture of kindness and cooperation. Instead of leaving people to struggle alone, they work as a team to find solutions that uplift everyone. **Ecclesiastes 4:9** tells us, *"Two are better than one because they have a good return for their labor."* Together, people can accomplish more than they ever could alone.

Solving problems is not just about making life easier; it is about helping others move forward. It is about offering a helping hand to someone who has fallen and reminding them that there is always a way out. **Psalm 46:1** reminds us, *"God is our refuge and strength, an ever-present help in trouble."* When we help solve problems, we reflect God's love and bring peace into someone's life

4. Strengthen

Strengthening others means uplifting them, reminding them of their worth, and helping them find courage when they feel weak. **Isaiah 41:10** says, *"Do not fear, for I am with you; do not be dismayed, for I am your God. I will strengthen you and help you."* We are called to strengthen others through love, faith, and encouragement.

Many people go through life feeling defeated, believing they are not strong enough to handle difficulties. But a simple word of encouragement can change everything. **Proverbs 27:17** says, *"As iron sharpens iron, so one person sharpens another."* We become stronger when we help others find their strength. Strength does not just come from physical power—it comes from the heart. A kind gesture, a supportive word, or even just standing beside someone in their struggles can be the strength they need. **1 Corinthians 16:13** reminds us, *"Be on your guard; stand firm in the faith; be courageous; be strong."* When we lift others up, we show them they are never alone.

5. Speak Well

The words we speak have power. They can build people up or tear them down. **Proverbs 18:21** says, *"The tongue has the power of life and death."* This means that what we say can either bring healing or harm. If we want to bless others, we must use words that encourage, uplift, and inspire.

Often, people speak harshly without considering how their words affect others. But when we choose kindness, we create an environment of love. **Ephesians 4:29** reminds us, *"Do not let any unwholesome talk come out of your mouths, but only what is helpful for building others up."* Every word we speak should be filled with positivity and grace.

Speaking well is not just about avoiding hurtful words—it is about actively using words that strengthen, empower, and bring joy. **Colossians 4:6** says, *"Let your conversation always be full of grace, seasoned with salt, so that you may know how to answer everyone."* Kind words can change lives, and the way we speak can be a powerful blessing to others.

SYAVIHA MULENGYA

6. Serve

Serving others is one of the greatest ways to show love and kindness. It means putting others before ourselves, helping those in need, and making a difference in the lives of people around us. **Mark 10:45** says, *"For even the Son of Man did not come to be served, but to serve, and to give His life as a ransom for many."* This verse reminds us that true greatness is found in serving others, not in seeking power or recognition.

Many people think that serving means doing big things, but even small acts of kindness matter. Helping a neighbor, listening to a friend, or giving to those in need are all ways to serve. **Galatians 5:13** tells us, *"Serve one another humbly in love."* Serving is not about showing off—it is about caring for others with a sincere heart.

Serving also brings joy. When we help others, we feel fulfilled and happy. It strengthens relationships and builds a world where people support one another. **Matthew 25:40** says, *"Whatever you did for one of the least of these brothers and sisters of mine, you did for me."* This means that every act of service, no matter how small, is valuable in God's eyes.

True service comes from the heart. It is not about expecting rewards or praise—it is about making life better for others. **1 Peter 4:10** reminds us, *"Each of you should use whatever gift you have received to serve others, as faithful stewards of God's grace."* When we serve with love, we create a world filled with kindness, unity, and compassion.

7. Sympathize

Sympathizing with others means understanding their pain, sharing in their struggles, and offering comfort. It is about showing kindness to those who are hurting and letting them know they are not alone. **Romans 12:15** says, "*Rejoice with those who rejoice; mourn with those who mourn.*" This verse teaches us that true love means standing with people in both their happy and difficult moments.

Many times, people suffer in silence because they feel no one understands them. But when we take time to listen and care, we bring healing. **Colossians 3:12** reminds us*, "Clothe yourselves with compassion, kindness, humility, gentleness, and patience."* Sympathy is not about fixing problems—it is about showing people that their feelings matter.

Sympathy also builds strong relationships. When we show understanding, we create trust and deepen connections. **2 Corinthians 1:3-4** says, "*Praise be to the God and Father of our Lord Jesus Christ, the Father of compassion and the God of all comfort, who comforts us in all our troubles, so that we can comfort those in any trouble.*" This means that when we receive comfort, we should also give comfort to others.

True sympathy comes from the heart. It is about being present, listening without judgment, and offering love without conditions. **Hebrews 13:1** reminds us, "*Keep on loving one another as brothers and sisters.*" When we sympathize with others, we create a world where people feel safe, valued, and support.

Do and Be Good

1. Superiority Shuts Souls

Some people see themselves as special because of status, skin, or success. They speak with pride, show off possessions, and silently look down on others. This spirit separates, stirs strife, and spoils relationships. Superiority steals the sweetness of serving. Jesus, the Savior, showed strength through surrender, not status. He sat with sinners, served the sick, and silenced self-righteousness. When we think we're better, we block blessings. We forget that every person is precious in God's plan. Pride pushes people away, but humility pulls hearts together. Superiority is a sickness that spreads silently. Healing begins when we honor others. → Who have you silently judged or avoided because they seemed "less?"

Superiority doesn't just hurt others—it hardens our own hearts. It makes us blind to beauty in broken places. It builds barriers instead of bridges. The Bible says to "value others above yourself" (**Philippians 2:3**). That means seeing worth in the weak, wisdom in the wounded, and wonder in the overlooked. When we stop seeking to shine, we start seeing souls. Humble hearts help heal homes, churches, and communities. Superiority says "me first," but humility says "you matter." We must shift from showing off to showing up. From being proud to being present. From being better to being a blessing. → What would change if you saw every person as equally loved by God?

Judgment

Judging others is easy—but it empties empathy. We jump to conclusions, joke about flaws, and justify our own faults. Judgment jabs like a knife, cutting connection and killing kindness. Jesus warned, *"Do not judge, or you too will be judged"* (**Matthew 7:1**). He didn't ignore sin—but He invited sinners to change through love. When we point fingers, we forget our own failures. Judgment makes us feel right but leaves others feeling rejected. It's a trap that turns truth into a tool for tearing down. Real love listens before it labels. It corrects with care, not cruelty. → Who have you criticized without understanding their story?

SYAVIHA MULENGYA

Joy grows when judgment goes. When we stop scanning for sin and start seeking souls, everything shifts. We become gentle, gracious, and grounded. We see people not as problems, but as possibilities. Jesus didn't shame the woman caught in sin—He showed her mercy (**John 8:11**). That's the model we must follow. Judgment divides, but grace draws people in. Let's replace harshness with healing and pride with patience. Let's be known not for pointing out faults, but for pouring out love. → What would your relationships look like if you led with grace instead of judgment?

Division Destroys Destiny

Division is deadly—it damages dreams and disconnects hearts. Pride, pain, and poor communication pull people apart. Families fight, friends fall out, and fellowships fracture. The devil delights in division because it weakens the witness of God's people. Jesus prayed for unity, not uniformity (**John 17:21**). He wanted believers to be bonded by love, not broken by ego. Division starts small—a sharp word, a silent grudge, a selfish choice. But it spreads fast and leaves deep scars. We must choose connection over conflict. → Who do you need to forgive to restore peace?

Destiny demands unity. We can't walk in purpose while warring with people. God calls us to be peacemakers, not peace-breakers. That means listening, learning, and letting go of pride. Love leads to healing, but hate holds us hostage. Division delays the good God wants to do through us. When we unite, we unlock strength. When we reconcile, we release revival. Don't let pride poison your path. Choose peace, pursue people, and protect unity. → What step can you take today to rebuild a broken relationship?

Blindness Blocks Blessing

Spiritual blindness makes us forget our need for mercy. We see others' mistakes but miss our own mess. We act holy but hide hurt. We preach truth but practice pride. **Romans 3:23** says, *"All have sinned and fall short of the glory of God."* That includes everyone—rich or poor, preacher or prisoner. Blindness builds walls of self-righteousness. It stops us from seeing the Savior's heart. Jesus saw the broken and brought them close. He didn't ignore sin, but He didn't ignore people either. → Are you seeing others through the eyes of grace or judgment?

Blessing begins with a clear vision. When we see ourselves rightly, we treat others kindly. We stop comparing and start caring. We stop boasting and start blessing. Spiritual sight shows us that grace is for all. It humbles the proud and lifts the lowly. Jesus opened blind eyes—and He still does today. Not just physical eyes, but spiritual ones. Let's ask God to help us see people as He sees them. With love, with hope, with mercy. → What would change if you truly believed everyone needs grace—including you?

Lord, You see every heart and know every motive. Forgive us for the times we've looked down on others—because of race, riches, roles, or religion. We've acted like we were above them, forgetting that we all stand level at the foot of the cross. Pride has poisoned our perspective and made us blind to our own brokenness. We've compared instead of cared, judged instead of joined, and criticized instead of connected. Help us to see people the way You do—with love, mercy, and value. Teach us to honor others, not because they've earned it, but because You created them. Break the spirit of superiority in us and build a spirit of humility. Let us serve, not shine; lift, not label; bless, not boast. Make us more like Jesus, who

SYAVIHA MULENGYA

chose the low place to lift others high. Today, we choose to walk humbly, love deeply, and live gently. Amen.

Prayer of Confession and Invitation to Jesus

Lord Jesus, I've tried to live my life my own way, and I confess—I've missed the mark. I've judged others, held onto pride, and walked far from Your truth. My heart has been heavy with guilt, and my soul has been searching for peace. Today, I admit that I need You—not just as a teacher, but as my Savior. I believe You died for my sins and rose again to give me new life. I ask You to forgive me, cleanse me, and change me from the inside out. Come into my heart, Jesus—not just for a moment, but forever. Be my Lord, my guide, and my closest friend. Teach me to love like You love, live like You lived, and walk in Your ways. Fill me with Your Spirit and lead me in truth. Thank You for Your mercy, Your grace, and Your promise to never leave me. From this day forward, I belong to You. Amen.

BY SYAVIHA MULENGYA

www.ingramcontent.com/pod-product-compliance
Lightning Source LLC
Chambersburg PA
CBHW071516120626
46550CB00006B/2246